Second Edition

SUCCESS GEMS

YOUR PERSONAL MOTIVATIONAL SUCCESS GUIDE

JEWEL DIAMOND TAYLOR

Foreword by
Iyanla Vanzant

1633 Bond Avenue
East Saint Louis, IL 62207

D0424342

Second Edition
Copyright © 1999 by Jewel Diamond Taylor
Previous edition copyrighted in 1995

Quiet Time Publishing
1633 Bond Avenue
East Saint Louis, Illinois 62207
t. 618.875-6808
f. 618.875-6809
e. QTpublish@aol.com
Los Angeles. 310.452-2922

Cover Design: Natalie Robinson
Editors: Toni L. Mathews, Roggie Wilson
A QTP/Balance Project

7 8 9 10 11 printing

Library of Congress Cataloging in Publication Data
Taylor, Jewel Diamond

ISBN 1884743 013

Dear reader, I dedicate these words and sentiments to you.
The world needs more dreamers like you... don't give up!

"No complaints and no regrets
I still believe in chasing dreams and placing bets.
And I have learned, when all you give... is all you get
so you give it all you got.

I had my share and drank my fill
and even though I'm satisfied
I'm hungry still.
You see what's down another road, beyond the hill
and do it all again.

So here's to life
and every joy it brings
Here's to life
to dreamers and their dreams.

Funny how the time just flies,
how love can go from warm hellos
to sad good-byes
and leave you with
the memories you memorize
to keep your winters warm.

But there's no "yes" in yesterday
and who knows what tomorrow brings or takes away.
As long as I'm still in the game
I want to play for laughs, for life or love.

May all your storms be weathered
and all that's good... get better.

Here's to life
and here's to love
and here's to YOU."

(lyrics sung by Joe Williams)

"There is gold and a multitude of rubies
but the lips of knowledge are a precious jewel."
Proverbs 10:15

CONTENTS

Foreword... 7
Acknowledgments... 9
Introduction... 11
Are You In The Diamond Lane?... 15
How Do You Spell Success?... 16
Self Inventory... 17
Self-Esteem Is Healthy not Selfish.... 18
Examine Yourself... 19
Your Sacred Self vs. Your Scared Self... 20
Be Inspired... 21
Decisions... 22
The Inner Eye Of A Winner... 23
Your Mission Needs A Vision... 24
How To Change Old Habits... 25
Check The B.S. In Your Life... 26
Cancel Your Pity Party... 27
Don't Sit On Your Assets... 28
Major Or Minor People... 30
You Are More Than Meets The Eye... 31
Do You Answer When Spirit Calls?... 32
You Are The Key... 33
What Are You Tuned Into?... 34
Do Your Inner Work... 35
Who Is The Author Of Your Story?... 36
Coping With Pressures In Life... 37
Negative Stress vs. Positive Stress... 38
Success And Survival... 39
Plugged In And Cordless... 40
Problems Or Pearls?... 41
The Greatest "Wait Loss" Program... 42
Reasons Why People Procrastinate... 43
How To Overcome Procrastination... 45
"Get It Done" Checklist... 46
Stay In The Light... 47
Around Every Flowering Tree Are Insects... 48
Attraction Power... 49

Health Is Wealth... 50
Comfort Zone... 51
Shift Happens... 52
Kiss My Positive Attitude... 53
Obedience To Your Purpose... 54
Knowledge Is Ecstasy... 55
Be A Good Manager... 56
The Power Of Ideas... 57
Entrepreneur Steps For Success... 58
Networking Works... 59
Four Answers... 60
Parenting Success... 61
Your Goals Are Your Children... 62
Cosmic Companionship... 63
Successful Relationships... 64
10 Things To Remember About Relationships... 65
Before You Get Married... 66
Seek Progress, Not Perfection... 68
7 Pearls For Daily Positive Prayer... 69
Diamonds In The Rough... 70
Get Even With Those Who Have Helped You... 71
Words Can Heal... 72
Words Can Harm And Hurt... 73
The Essence Of Gemstones... 74
Vocabulary For Success... 75
Gemology... 76
The Main Thing... 77
40 Valuable Lessons That I've Learned... 78
10 Steps For Success... 80
Find Your Zone... 82
Who's Shaping Your Thoughts?... 83
Is Your Life Out Of Balance?... 84
Enjoy Your Life... 85
Are You Ignoring God's Help?... 86
Jewel's Poetry Gems... 87
Diamond Affirmations... 105
Diamond Quotations... 115
My Favorite Quotes From Past And Present... 124

FOREWORD

Within each of us, there is a precious "Gem" waiting to be discovered. That gem is a thing of beauty, of great worth, of extreme value and distinction. You are a diamond in the rough. Pressure makes diamonds. Each unrefined jewel, must be found, dug up, cleaned off and pressured into a state of value. When we do not realize the value of what is buried within us, how precious we are, we crumble under the pressure of life. The pressure of fear, guilt, shame, blame, the struggle for power and control. Until today! Today and every day that you take the time to dig through this work, to apply the prescriptions to your life, you come closer to sharpening your points, rounding your edges, polishing your surface, displaying yourself as the priceless jewel you were created to be.

Jewel Diamond Taylor has withstood the pressures of life. She knows her value, her worth. Like any other jewel of great worth and value, she is shining in the showcase of life. She is shining her light on the world with the "Gems" she shares in this work. She has your attention, your interest. You are thumbing through this work wondering if you can afford to pick it up. If you are experiencing any of the pressures of life, you cannot afford not to embrace this work. Sister Jewel is an expert "gemologist," fully capable of molding and shaping your mind and your spirit into a state of great value.

No one wants to suffer. No one wants to live in pain. No one elects to live through the dulling confusion of valuelessness, worthlessness and self denial. Unfortunately, our indoctrination into this life creates the illusion: there is something we must *have,* in order to *do* and ultimately we can *be,* a thing of great worth and value. Until today! Today, as you begin the process of digging into yourself, you will realize, there is nothing for you to do but to do! You *are* the very thing you seek. You are your perfect health, your peace, your joy, your wealth. If you can, in your heart, mind and body, "*Be*" what you want, you can *Do* what you desire and *Have* what you want. *Be! Do! Have*! That is the process of self discovery, of refining the gem that you already are.

Purpose plus *Power* equals *Success*. When you tap into your purpose, the reason you were born, you are imbued with power; you begin to shine. When you realize you are powerful and valuable, you become focused. Focus brings clarity, determination and commitment. Commitment is the seed of success. That is what "Gems" is about. It is your stimulation to be your success, without fear, doubt or hesitation. It is the formula by which you can understand and withstand the pressures of life. As you make the commitment to incorporate these Gems into your life, you are bound to realize your purpose; you will undoubtedly find your power; you will realize the keys to your success.

I am excited for you! I can hardly wait to see the glitter and glimmer of precious Gems, moving throughout the world, shining through life's pressures, emitting rays of light. There is nothing more exciting than walking into a jewelry store realizing you can afford to have anything you want! I am in the jewelry store of life, waiting for my fellow Gems to show up and show themselves off!

Iyanla Vanzant

ACKNOWLEDGMENTS

I acknowledge my Creator and Lord God for the realization of my goal and ideas for this book. I am thankful and humbled by the talents, blessings, love, grace and opportunities given to me.

Thank you God for choosing me to be loved by so many. Thank you for the memories and strength of my ancestors. My family life, career life and this book have been a labor of love. I give thanks for the success it brings to everyone involved in its publication. I give thanks for the success it brings to those who read, apply and share the knowledge.

I am thankful to be a channel of inspiration in bringing myself, my loved ones and readers of this book closer to the knowledge of God and their greater Self. My prayer is to not only be a great teacher and speaker, but to have the courage and integrity to live by my own words.

I acknowledge God as my Source and give thanks for the reSources in my life that bring me comfort, health, joy, friendship, success, prosperity and understanding.

There have been many times when I have been divorced from my divinity. In my quest for love and truth, I discovered my purpose and a way to become united again with the Spirit without apology or hesitation. I choose to continue to grow spiritually, mentally, physically and emotionally.

Words cannot fully express what I feel in gratitude and joy to have the opportunity to present SUCCESS GEMS to the world. This book is my living testimony that putting God first in your life is a prerequisite for success in all areas of your life.

May those in darkness, come to know YOUR love and light and shine as the precious jewels they were created to be in MIND, BODY and SPIRIT.

In spite of any seeming obstacles or fear, my vow is to continually STAY in YOUR LIGHT!

And so it IS!

My family and friends have provided me with unspeakable joy, love and support. So many faces and names are to be remembered and thanked. I must give thanks to the ones listed.

"You have given me love and support in countless ways. Each of you know the special contribution and difference you have made in my life. May you always know my love and heartfelt gratitude. Thank you for believing in me."

TO MY FAMILY

John, JJ, Jason, Joy, Neil, Pops, Jamila, Greg, Aunt Louise, Uncle Johnny, Serena & Uncle Charles

TO MY FRIENDS

Bayyinah Ali Shotwell, Tracy Kennedy, Deborah Granger, Iyanla Vanzant, Maria Carothers, Gigi Garcia, Mark Cargill, Dalton Wilson, Debrena Jackson-Gandy, Bonnie R. Fells, Valesha Carter, Patrizia Glenn, Norma Blinks, Asha Bell, Monique Hunter, Beah Richards, Nadine McKinnor, Tim Morrow, William Drake, Sylvester Rivers, Rico Reed, Vera Walston, Kim Thompson, Cynthia Jackson, Kim Harden, Norman and Theresa Golden, Cynthia Stokes, Lady Prema, and The Mooney Twins.

"You were there when I needed a friend, a ride, money, your professional service, career referral, mentoring, volunteers, companionship, a prayer and support as I grew personally and professionally. Thank you."

*And **thanks to all the participants** in my **Enlightened Circle Seminars** for the past 7 years. Each of you were invaluable to my professional growth and personal healing while serving in the public. You allowed me the freedom to be myself. You allowed me to teach and learn at the same time. I wish I could list all your names. I hope you will have a copy of this book to feel and know my appreciation.*

You are all precious jewels in my "jewelry box of life." May you know God's greatness and goodness for you always. Stay in His Light."

INTRODUCTION

Dear reader, the following pages are precious touchstones from me to you. My intention is to share insight through motivational messages, positive affirmations, quotations and metaphors of the diamond.

My father was a jeweler in Washington D.C. where I was born in 1951. I was the first born of three girls. I am thankful my parents bestowed me with a name of radiance as a legacy to my father's successful business. After my father's passing, I began to study his gemology books and became intrigued with the lessons gems can impart. Most of the diamonds on the planet come from my Motherland Africa.

The diamond contains all the attributes and qualities toward a perfected state in the mineral kingdom. The diamond is a chunk of coal which through countless polishings and friction acquires its incredible brilliance. It is the strongest element in the earth. We can learn from this.

Everything created comes from darkness into light. The darkness can be the vastness of the universe, the womb of Mother Earth, the diamond emerging from black coal, personal revelations and insight after dark experiences such as a loss of a loved one, loss of a job, sickness, financial setback, recovery from an addiction or a relationship that ends. These unwanted and unexpected dark times bring forth lessons, increase your strength to endure and very often bring new relationships, a new understanding, new opportunities and a new perception of this thing called "life."

I believe we are like diamonds undergoing cutting, polishing, pressure and friction. We have many processes and lessons to grow through before we reach a state of beauty and brilliance.

The first part of the book offers power thoughts, questions and suggestions to stimulate your mind. These are excerpts from my professional career as a workshop presenter, keynote speaker and personal transformation counselor. I am a speaker first and writer second. So it was a real challenge to discipline myself to sit down and condense a hour presentation or class series onto one page. My intention was to present ideas that you could read on one page during your break at work, sitting in a waiting room, or when you arise in the morning as a quick mental boost.

If you belong to a support/study group, prayer group or master-mind group, these one page gems are excellent for group discussion. I have selected topics from my speeches and Enlightened Circle classes that have received the most popular responses.

One approach to this book would be to select one "gem" for the week. Focus on it. Analyze and apply what principles you need from that particular lesson to improve your life. Or choose one per day as your guidepost to keep you motivated throughout the day.

If you are a teacher, select one of the "gems" for your class discussion. Young people can benefit greatly from the metaphors and ideas for success and endurance to improve their critical thinking and goal-setting skills.

As a concerned parent, you can introduce your child to the world of positive thinking to help enhance their self-esteem, reading skills and optimism for their future.

In any case, these pages can be a source of light to the reader who seeks clarity and new insights for living, thinking and achieving.

The second part of the book provides positive affirmations to develop strong inner fitness. The mind and body are not separate. Our dominant thoughts affect our health, wealth, happiness, peace and quality of life. In this section, I offer affirmations for you to read and affirm for your life. When you decide to commit to a pro-gram for "inner fitness," you will **exercise** your faith, **jump** for joy, **run** with patience, **push up** your discipline, **lift** your attitude and **reduce the weight** of stress and fear.

These affirmations are like **lifting** mental weights to strengthen your self-esteem and self-determination. They keep you from being weak when criticism, changes or disappointments occur in your life. Exercise as much as possible for your inner fitness with the affirma-tions for money, health, coping with change, building self-esteem and strengthening your spiritual muscles to survive and win your personal battles.

I believe we are created with the ability to receive ideas, dwell upon them and carry them forth into expression.

The last part of *SUCCESS GEMS* offers some of my quotes from my seminars and keynote presentations for success building, learning how to be focused and never wanting to give up! Some of them have been my own personal themes to keep me motivated and help overcome the temptation to stop just because I was getting pebbles in my shoes climbing the mountain of success. Many times I have to remind myself to stay focused and that "The main thing is to keep the Main Thing... the MAIN THING!"

I have also listed some of my favorite quotes of people in the past and present collected over the years from my reading and study. These minds have inspired and assisted me in my mental and spiritual shifts for deeper understanding. As I compiled them for you, I was again energized and motivated by the profound but simply stated truths that transcend time and space. May you be inspired by them, too, in your personal transformation.

I have come to understand that I am a spiritual being having a human experience. My human experience has given birth to poetry from my pain and pleasure. As the Mother of these poems, I share with pride a few selected poems of mine at the end of the book.

These are my gems to share: success lessons for your tests in life, affirmations, quotations and poetry. The quality of your life is in your hands. The management of your life is in your hands. Your destiny is in your hands. Your success is in your hands. Now my book is in your hands. There are no accidents in the universe. Divine order is always taking place. So value them and polish them up for your use.

With love, faith, self-esteem, nurturing relationships and a willingness to grow and act on your dreams... we cease being "diamonds in the rough." This book project is my way of opening up my "jewelry box of life," offering my pearls of wisdom from experience and study. May they assist you in your personal growth and daily leaps of faith for greater success and fulfillment in your life. Ready, set and glow!

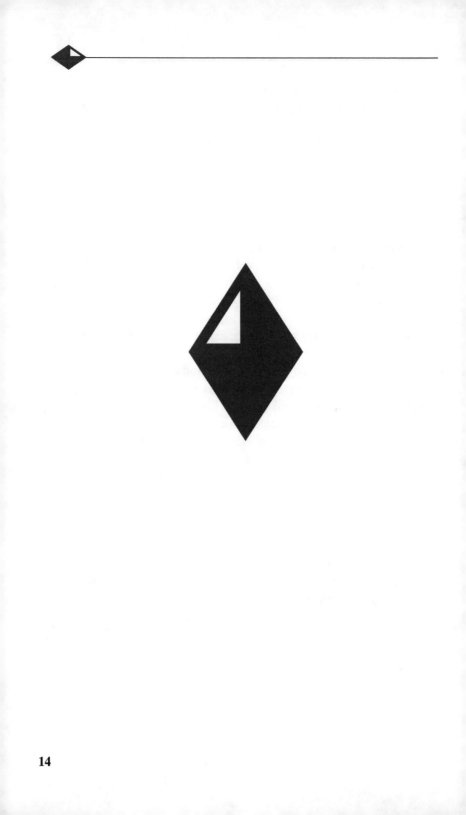

ARE YOU IN THE DIAMOND LANE?

I live in Southern California where there are lots of people, cars and freeways. The "diamond lane" is the designated commuter lane. It is an incentive for two or more commuters to help shorten their driving time and reduce traffic jams and pollution. Whenever I'm in the "diamond lane," I arrive at my destination faster and I have someone sharing my journey with me, desiring the same destination. We have the opportunity to talk and share and my journey seems less of a hassle.

In life's journey, traveling the "diamond lane" sometimes will help you arrive at your goal faster. Who do you spend most of your time with? Who supports you in accomplishing your goals? Are you struggling alone, stuck in the "traffic jam of life" and getting nowhere fast? Are you in the slow lane of life or are you in the fast lane, headed for an accident?

Yes, there are times you need to travel alone but there's a difference between being alone and being lonely. There are times when having other people in your "car of life" will slow you down. They may be back-seat drivers and tell you how to live your life. Sometimes people with no goals or maps of their own will talk you into getting off your highway to go their way.

When you find like-minded people moving and growing in your same direction... get in the "diamond lane." Share, network, spend time together, support one another and you'll reach your destination much quicker. You will pass up the other traffic of people who want to go it alone, stuck on ego, not willing to share, afraid to connect, moving too slow or simply lost with no direction.

Life is a journey. Your key to get started is your faith. Your goals are your map. Your vehicle is your body. Your fuel is your nutrition. You are in the driver's seat controlling your life, or you are a passenger letting someone else make your decisions. All of these factors, including your co-journers, determine the quality of your journey. A successful trip requires regular tune-ups, so take care of yourself. Enjoy the scenery of life. Sometimes there are detours or setbacks. Just remember to get back on your highway again. Read and adhere to warning signs. Go with the flow of traffic. Don't stress out when temporary traffic jams occur. Travel in the "diamond lane" whenever possible.

HOW DO YOU SPELL SUCCESS?

Success means different things to different people. For people in underdeveloped countries, success could be spelled FOOD or WATER. Homeless people, displaced and feeling invisible, may spell success SHELTER, WARMTH, or JOB.

People who have known poverty and struggle all their life may spell success as MONEY. People who have known oppression may spell success as FREEDOM or POWER. People who have known sickness may spell success as HEALTH. People choosing to have a family may spell success GOOD PARENTING, or GOOD PROVIDER.

People struggling each day with drug or alcohol abuse may spell success RECOVERY. Or someone working at an unfulfilling and unchallenging job may spell success SELF EMPLOYED. A student may spell success SCHOLARSHIP or COLLEGE DEGREE. A poet or writer may spell success PUBLISHER. A person tired of being alone may spell success LOVE. A person overcoming depression may spell success INNER PEACE. A single parent may spell success as FINANCIAL SUPPORT. A person riding the bus may spell success as CAR. An entrepreneur may spell success as MORE CUSTOMERS. A musician may spell success as RECORD DEAL.

How do you spell success? Do you let society, the media, your parents, your peers or your mate define what success means to you? Success isn't always measured in money or status. Your success may never receive an award or be on the front page of a newspaper. What is important to you right now? Is it better health, inner peace, a new car, a happy family, a thriving business, new friends, stronger faith or traveling? Do you want to return to school, have a divine and loving relationship or send your child to college? Do you want to start a business, heal a relationship or enhance your wardrobe? Do you want to start exercising, quit smoking or end a toxic relationship? Do you want to write your book, work in your community or get a new look? Define success for yourself and begin to do what it takes to achieve it. Success is not like a dress... one size does not fit all. Don't compare yourself to others. Be true to yourself.

SELF-INVENTORY

We are multifaceted and have human flaws just as the diamond is multifaceted and has flaws. We must not focus on our flaws. Instead, we must seek daily within ourselves to discern that we are not operating from a **negative** self-will which creates **havoc** in our lives. Self-inventory will help us determine if we are operating from the **positive** center of God's will which will create **harmony** in our lives.

Negative Self-Will	Positive God's Will
selfish/self-seeking	interest in others
dishonesty	honesty
frightened	courage
inconsiderate	considerate
pride	humility
greed	giving or sharing
anger	calm
envy	grateful
sloth/lazy	taking action
reactive	pro-active
gluttony	moderation
impatience	patience
intolerance	tolerance
resentment	forgiveness
hate	love
harmful acts	good deeds
self-pity	self-forgetfulness
self-importance	modesty
self-condemnation	self-forgiveness
suspicion	trust
doubt	faith
stubborn	willing
confusion/disorder	harmony
lustful	loving

SELF-ESTEEM IS HEALTHY not SELFISH

When I was studying human behavior in my psychology studies at California University, Dominguez Hills in the 70's, the phrases "inferiority" and "superiority complex" referred to the varying degrees of one's self-perception. Now, in the 90's, the buzz words are "low or high self-esteem."

Self-esteem reflects one's sense of value, worth, confidence, self-acceptance and self-appreciation/love.

One extreme of self-esteem can be acting arrogant, cocky or egotistical and "full of one's self." The opposite extreme would be suicidal, hopeless, a sense of no worth or value. One needs a "healthy" self-esteem to be successful in his or her chosen career. One also needs to diffuse messages from media, society and toxic/negative people that would attempt to strip one of his or her inherent beauty and pursuit of individual expression.

As you strive for more fulfillment and success in your life you may be challenged or attacked.

"Why are you doing that?"
"Who do you think your are?"
"I remember your past failures."
"You're too stupid, ugly, fat, broke, old, handicapped,
  untalented."
"You can't make a living doing that!"
"Why don't you be normal like everybody else."

Continue believing in yourself even when nobody else will. Learn how to be your own best friend and cheerleader. Learn how to say "no" to toxic people and situations that bring you down or drain you of enthusiasm and conviction towards your highest good and goal. I share a poem on page 88 that I wrote as I healed from low self-esteem and learned to trust and believe in myself and my abilities.

EXAMINE YOURSELF

I believe there are three nagging questions that haunt us. Our deepest desire is that the answer would always be "yes." "**Did** I do the right thing?... Am I doing the right thing **now?**... **Will** I do the right thing?"

In my own personal journey of self-discovery and healing, I've had to ask and answer these questions. I discovered people were motivated to attend my Enlightened Circle seminars and retreats over the years because they found themselves asking the same questions seeking guidance and support. Together we learned we were restless and wanted more out of life.

Realizing you haven't lived up to your potential or that you let a dream die is painful. Certain scriptures spoke to me to jolt me out of procrastination and denial.

Corinthians challenged me by stating
"examine yourself."

The Book of Timothy encouraged me to
"Stir up the gift that is in thee."

In order to examine yourself and pursue your worthy goal of accomplishing something and a meaningful life... begin by asking yourself these questions:

1. Are you excited to get up in the morning?
2. What are you happy about in your life now?
3. Do you have a purpose in your life to which you are committed?
4. What are you proud about in your life?
5. What are you grateful for in your life?
6. Who do you love and who loves you?
7. Who or what do you give most of your time to?
8. What did you learn today?
9. What fears, guilt, anger or shame are you holding onto?
10. Are you satisfied with your income?
11. Are you using your talents and abilities?
12. Do you feel your work is rewarding?
13. What is your guiding philosophy in life?
14. Do you like where you are living?
15. Are you happy with your body and health?
16. Do you look forward to the future with confidence?

YOUR SACRED SELF vs. YOUR SCARED SELF

Loving, respecting and honoring God is your "significant other" relationship. Learning to communicate, trust and joyfully surrender to God's will is developed through your:

> spiritual education
> meditation and prayer
> atonement (at one ment)
> illumination
> oblation
> devotion
> obedience

Your daily spiritual walk, not just on Sundays, will help you discover your **sacred** self, while the old **scared** self dies. The scared self plays games with others, hurts self and others and doesn't experience love. The scared self knows all about pain, doubt and fear.

The sacred self experiences the love of God and a love for God, self and others. The Divine above and within makes you feel one with the world, not separate.

Honoring your sacred self means giving your body (temple) the food, exercise and rest it needs. It means listening to your feelings and asking others for what you deserve without feeling guilty.

Loving yourself means learning how to esteem yourself and recognize your worthiness. Pat yourself on the back for your strength and past successes. Being a good parent and provider is success. You are a success because of the quiet deeds of kindness you give to others asking nothing in return. That is success. You have endured pain and been unselfish many times. That is success. You have served your organization or community well as a "behind the scenes" person, with little or no recognition. However, you are still a success because of your dependability and generous giving of time, talent and energy.

Acknowledge your past successes. Remove and rescue yourself from negative/abusive situations that make you scared. Your sacred self will give you the gift of massage, flowers, quiet time, take yourself to dinner or vacation. Your sacred self will always return you to sanity and serenity.

BE INSPIRED

Don't get discouraged easily by life's trials and tribulations. Just open your eyes, heart, ears and mind. When you do, you will hear positive messages in music like Sounds of Blackness, the laughter of a child or a bird in a tree. You can be inspired by so many who have turned their obstacles into opportunities. Listen to the stories of your elders of how they coped and didn't give up hope. They endured harsher times fighting for dignity, progress and equality.

Be inspired by authors who tell their stories of visions, valleys and victories like: Iyanla Vanzant, author of "Acts of Faith" and "Tapping The Power Within"; Dennis Kimbro, author of "Think And Grow Rich: A Black Choice"; Les Brown, author of "Live Your Dreams"; John Johnson, author of "Succeeding Against All Odds"; George Fraser, author of "Success Runs In Our Race"; any of Jawanza Kunjufu's books; "Message to the People," by Marcus Garvey; Susan Taylor's book, "In the Spirit" or her weekly articles in *Essence Magazine*, or Queen Afua's book "Heal Thyself."

Be inspired by the crossing guard in your neighborhood who serves our children with joy and dependability. Read your local newspapers to applaud the efforts of local sheroes and heroes who are fighting and winning battles for better social conditions. Be inspired by the educators who continue to teach under stressful conditions. Be inspired by volunteers who care for the underserved in our community. Be inspired by the increasing number of entrepreneurs who succeed and must compete with larger budgets and companies. Be inspired by the artists who paint, create and design using colors, fabrics and nature. Be inspired by Nelson Mandela and Winnie Mandela's life of sacrifice, struggle and victory. Be inspired by your children's curiosity and intelligent minds. Be inspired by loving parents successfully raising their children. Be inspired by those who got up when they were told to sit down. Be inspired by those who were told they would not **become** worth anything... but they succeeded to **overcome** other's judgement of them. Be inspired by the new film directors, producers, actors and actresses who bring truth, talent and integrity to the screen. Be inspired by the visionaries who don't settle for just being ordinary.

Inspiration is all <u>around</u> you, it is <u>in</u> you and <u>for</u> you. It is <u>up to you</u>. Inhale and exhale. Breathe in all the positive energy and the Spirit of the universe to in-spire and enrich your life.

DECISIONS

The success of parents, leaders, managers, health care givers, educators, visionaries, entrepreneurs and policy makers is determined by their ability to make decisions. All of us need to learn to be successful in making decisions because to better manage our lives requires better decision making.

Sometimes businesses like restaurants close down and then re-open with signs stating, "under new management." In most cases the old management style failed. In order to turn the business around and realize a profit, new management comes in with new ideas, new energy, new vision, new attitude and new style of approaching an old problem.

What happens when you realize your best thinking has gotten you this far, and this far isn't good enough? Maybe your life isn't being managed well and you want your life to be more successful. Perhaps it's time for "new management."

Building your life under "new management" requires you to observe how you make decisions. You'll have to "fire" and let go of the character habits that didn't serve you well. Evaluate your goals, your attitude and your resources.

Decisions are based on two things... 1) your <u>memories</u> of past failures or successes and 2) your <u>faith</u> in possibilities yet unseen.

In the past, your decisions were based on fear because you remembered past mistakes or pain. Or your memory reminds you of what you did before successfully, so you think you can do it again.

Faith teaches you to rise above past limitations and believe you can accomplish new goals. Education, self-esteem and spiritual realization will improve your new management style. The more you learn about your business, the more you can earn. Discover what you are lacking. Knowledge begets confidence and confidence begets wise action. Spiritual study and obedience begets faith, faith begets trust and trust begets strong belief in positive outcomes. You can make wiser decisions based on what you strongly believe, know and expect. New management requires courage, optimism, determination to win and willingness to lead and decide.

THE *INNER* EYE OF A WINNER

Be like a w**inner** who uses their **inner** eye to see beyond temporary roadblocks. The **inner** eye doesn't judge by appearances only. A determined w**inner** keeps their eye on the goal.

The sculptor uses the **inner** eye of insight to see possibilities in a slab of marble that the untrained eye can't see. A gemologist sees with the **inner** eye a diamond inside a chunk of coal. A seamstress' **inner** eye sees a beautiful dress while looking at a piece of uncut fabric. A mother determined to feed her family on a limited budget can stretch one package of meat into many different tasty dishes.

The sculptor, gemologist, seamstress and mother see with their insight many possibilities that a shortsighted person wouldn't see. The more they use the **inner** eye of creativity the stronger it becomes.

The **inner** eye of a laid off aerospace worker can see a layoff as an opportunity to pursue an old dream of starting their own business, shift careers or update skills/education. The **inner** eye sees an illness as an opportunity to value their health and become more committed to a healthier life-style of eating, exercise and reduced stress. The **inner** eye sees a failed relationship as an opportunity to get to know self, meet their own needs and learn how to make one's self happy **first** before getting involved in another toxic, dependent or immature relationship.

How you **see** yourself, your problems or possibilities shape your perception. Your perception is your mental image, awareness and intuitive cognition. Check your (perception) **inner vision.** How far can you **see** into your future? What do you **see** in yourself? How do you **see** your problems affecting you <u>or</u> stopping you? Do you **see** your opportunities? Are you **blind** with anger, jealousy or self-defeat? Do you **see** the lesson in your pain? Do you **see** things in your life getting better? Do you **see** God active in your life? Do you **see** your hidden talents and strengths? Hind**sight** gives you guidelines and wisdom from your past. Fore**sight** is your ability to prepare for the future. In**sight** is your intuition. Your perception of self and ability to act is very key in your desire to be successful in life. To complete your mission... check your vision!

YOUR MISSION NEEDS A VISION

We are motivated and conditioned by our 5 senses of smell, touch, sight, hearing and taste. Since we are creatures of habit, a lot of our decisions, actions and expectations in life are governed by our senses. The subconscious is non-judgemental. So whether an experience is positive or negative, bitter or sweet, pleasant or painful, loud or soft... we are conditioned by past experiences and memory to want what is familiar to our senses.

Visual stimulation is proven to be a strong motivator. If you want to introduce new experiences into your life, repeated visual stimulation can be successful.

Two strategies are recommended for successfully reaching your goals.

1. I have a "vision board" in my office. It has words and pictures of goals I need to act upon. It keeps me focused and inspires me to keep going in spite of setbacks. The words are written boldly and big. The words are action-oriented. I write the words of projects and ideas on the board. I also have the words "Thank you" on the board. My faith guides me to be thankful before I even reach my good.

    Your vision board can be on a bulletin board, a wall, re-frigerator door or on the back of a door in your room.

2. I have a "treasure map". This is a photo album book filled with pictures and words cut out from magazines. This book is my visual motivation of the people, places, things, travel, prosperity, family and ideas I want to acquire and/or main-tain in my life. I have pictures of family, health, food, travel, airplanes, vacations, office equipment, furniture, poetry, pictures of my public speaking, retreats and beautiful homes.

    When you make your treasure map, use a lot of color. Use your imagination. Have fun with it. This exercise helps your creativity and imagination. It can inspire you to be-come more specific and committed to your dreams and goals.

HOW TO CHANGE OLD HABITS

It's common to hear the phrase, "we are creatures of habit." The word creature is derived from the word "create." Yes, we do create through our words, actions, feelings, mind, memories and habits. We create stress or success, havoc or happiness. We can create a job, a business, a relationship, a drug habit, a spending habit, or illness. We can create love, music, a book, art, peace, a new building or new invention.

A good analogy of understanding our habits is the computer. Your mind is more powerful than a computer. Your mind can store more information than a computer. The similarity is that just like a computer, your mind accepts the "input." You allow messages into your mind from parents, teachers, friends, TV, radio, movies, magazines, lovers, husband, wife, books, co-workers, childhood memories, positive and negative experiences. This is your data on your floppy disk. Your internal program determines your perception, self-esteem and subsequently your behavior.

When someone or some circumstance pushes your emotional button, your response or feelings show up on your "screen of life." What comes on the screen is determined by the input, data (your subconscious and your consciousness). If the input is dominantly positive, your life will project that. If your input is dominantly negative, your life will project that. "Garbage in... garbage out." As within, so without. Your mind received the data (impressions) then your life produced the printout (expressions). You cannot feel and act positive, if the data is not stored in your memory (subconscious). If you desire to change the "program" of your life, know that you are the "programmer." You will need to "install" affirmations and knowledge and "delete" some habits and/or relationships. You will need to set new "margins" to think higher and bigger. You will need to "center" yourself through spiritual meditation and study.

I know it's not as simple as 1...2...3... Overriding previous negative messages and impressions take time. First you have to <u>unlearn</u> before you learn new ways. Self-observation and self-correction are the key. Be committed to the process of positive change in your life. You are a creature of habit. Observe which old habits are controlling your life. You <u>can</u> break the old habits. You are the programmer.

CHECK THE B.S. IN YOUR LIFE

A child is born innocent, trusting, loving and with a rich imagination. A child will believe Superman can really fly and that Santa Claus comes down the chimney if that is his/her indoctrination. A child's ability to learn, dream, trust, excel and explore are encouraged or discouraged during these early years. The child's consciousness is continually being shaped into adolescence and onto adulthood by continuing memories, myths and messages from family, school, environment, peers, society, their culture and lessons learned from painful mistakes or rewarding successes. Subsequently, the belief system (B.S.) of this person has been formed and becomes the guiding force in their life. Decisions, judgements, reactions, actions, habits, feelings, thoughts of limitation or aspirations for the highest are determined by your B.S. (belief system).

A bad experience in school, being told you wouldn't amount to anything, a failed relationship or failed business venture, and an environment that doesn't nurture hope, education, self-reliance or creativity can shape your B.S. The belief system shaped will be based on limitation and low expectations from self and life.

Check your B.S. Have you learned to limit yourself? Do you still dream? Do you believe you can change your present circumstances for the better? Do you believe that some people are just lucky, smarter, prettier, faster or more worthy than you? Do you believe it's too late to start again? Are you afraid of failure or rejection because of the past? Are you feeling like a hopeless victim because you don't see anyone in your environment rising above and overcoming negative conditions?

"What you **believe determines** what you can **achieve**." Be willing to read, leave your comfort zone, open up to new ideas, new places and new people. Believe again as a child, in the impossible. **Faith, imagination, self-esteem and determination** help you to see the invisible, reach the untouchable, bear the unbearable, believe the unbelievable and conquer the immovable. The Bible's wisdom reminds us, "it is done unto you as you believe." Check your B.S. Who taught you to be afraid? Don't let an old belief system keep you from succeeding in a new relationship, a new career, financial freedom or that new business/project you desire.

CANCEL YOUR PITY PARTY

Worrying and feeling sorry for yourself only changes one thing... YOU. Worry and self-pity don't change the circumstances. Worry and self-pity are self-inflicted forms of stress. Continually talking and focusing your attention on your pain are a misuse of your time and energy.

Some people unknowningly create, promote, allow or expect problems knocking on their door. Sometimes the challenge of solving a problem, the attention they receive or the drama of problems have a strange familiar appeal.

The only people that will accept your invitations to your "pity party" are those who prolong and perpetuate your agony because they really don't care, glad to know someone else has problems or secretly thinking, "I'm glad it's not me."

I have learned the value of only sharing my challenges and times of uncertainty with those people who are positive, spiritual and who are a part of the solution.

I discovered very quickly that negative people like to be with negative people. The conversation of negative people is negative and focused on doom and gloom. Their words and outlook have a powerful affect on you, if you allow yourself to be in their presence too long.

I also discovered that positive people like to be with positive people. The conversation of positive people is positive and focused on solutions, optimism and faith. Their words and positive outlook have a powerful affect on you if you allow yourself to be in their presence.

My "pity parties" are short lived now because I have intentionally surrounded myself with positive support and a spiritual foundation.

To reduce your "pity parties" focus on these four "A"s each day. Choose your **Attitude** for the day. Don't let anyone or anything conquer you. Try to be pleasant, peaceful and positive. Choose your **Agenda** (priorities, things to accomplish). Take **Action** and don't procrastinate because action empowers you. Choose who you **Associate** with carefully. Learn how to discern between negative and positive people.

DON'T SIT ON YOUR ASSETS

Diamonds can be overlooked as a piece of rock or chunk of coal. The same is true for opportunities. An opportunity can be overlooked by the untrained eye or the person not determined enough to discover their success.

Are you sitting on your assets? Are you asking for help, customers, love, money, a job, a car or a new place to live, but feel you are at a dead end? Resources, people and ideas are all around you. Who do you know?

your family	your friends
who is retired	what business cards do you have
who reads books on success	who cuts your hair
who works at your bank	who does your nails
who manages your building	who sold you your car
who do you meet in the store	who is wealthy
who is the receptionist	who is in the newspaper
where did you live before	who is active in your school
who likes to talk	what about your child's school
who did you meet at a party	who attends seminars
who do you know at church	who did you meet on vacation
who bought a new home	who did you meet at a conference
who do you know in fund raising	who do you know in politics
who repairs your house	who likes to buy and shop
who likes to network	who is in the Chamber of Commerce
who has lots of friends	who are out of town relatives
who is in your phone book	who is active in the community
who is your boss	who is your former boss
who are your co-workers	who are your former co-workers
who is in your social organization	who is in your neighborhood
who is your doctor, dentist	who calls you at home
who just started a new business	who is the teacher/principal
who is your mentor	who is your minister

Once you become focused and motivated, you will turn over every stone. You will seek answers, customers, referrals and support from unfamiliar places. Don't miss a great opportunity because you misjudge a person or an organization. Don't underestimate yourself.

Your faith, intelligence, past experience, courage, willingness, self-esteem, creativity and persistence are assets. Don't minimize your strengths. Don't be afraid to ASK for what you want. ASK for the business. ASK for the sale. ASK for the loan/grant/scholarship. ASK for the job. ASK for support.

MAJOR OR MINOR PEOPLE

I remember hearing once that the two things that will change your life five years from now are the books you read and the people you meet. I have found that to be very true. I invest in myself by purchasing and reading books. I have benefited richly from the pearls of wisdom imparted by teachers and authors. The knowledge acquired has reshaped my perception and goals in life. I have more confidence and I feel better prepared to overcome obstacles. Knowledge is power.

Successfully growing in my personal and professional life required me to let go of certain relationships and develop new relationships. My phone book changed as I changed. I quickly learned to discern between major and minor people. There are some people who only want to gossip, complain, whine, manipulate, be negative and unproductive, have no ambition and no vision or simply full of fear and have low self-esteem. These are jewels who have lost their luster, brilliance and are not shining their light.

Then there are those jewels in life that are creative, brilliant, sparkling, shining, positive, productive, supportive and overcoming their flaws. These are major people. Their attitudes and life-styles are contagious.

Most of my audiences will hear me say: "Don't spend major time with minor people and don't spend minor time with major people. Understand the power and influence people have that can decrease or increase the quality of your life. No one has a neutral affect on you. Associating with the wrong people can change your life and associating with the right people can also change your life. It's up to you to choose."

Who are the major people in your life that can make a positive difference in your life? Do you spend enough time with them? Do you write or call them? Do you balance your life with family, friends and professional relationships? Have you read the books of successful people and educators? Have you attended their meetings or seminars? Look at your phone book. Have you met any new people recently?

Always remember, creative people like to be with creative people. Successful people like to be with successful people. Healthy people like to be with healthy people. Positive people like to be with positive people.

YOU ARE MORE THAN MEETS THE EYE

You are tri-dimensional. You came from the spirit. Therefore, you are a spirit (spiritual/soul). Your spirit is housed in a body (physical). Your body is animated by the mind (mental). Your 5 senses in the mind interpret your world. The spirit, mind and body are ONE. Each dimension affects the other. This is the whole (holy) trinity (tri=three; u(nity) unified).

Acknowledging, honoring and tapping into this unified power helps you to release blame, live without judging, give up struggling and joyfully surrender to the Divine Will for your life. Your fears, guilt and anger generate from your MIND. Your cravings, desires and obsessions generate from your BODY. Your values and ambitions generate from your SPIRIT. When you are conscious of your tri-dimensional self, it helps to diminish confusion and limited living.

For the whole person to be healthy, the mind needs to be developed and free of toxic thoughts. The body has to be nurtured, strengthened and free of toxic foods. The spiritual self has to be developed and have a heightened awareness of its inherent power. If any one of the three bodies are not at their optimal performance, it affects the other levels of performance. If the faith is strong in your spiritual self, the physical body has a greater chance of healing. If the physical body is strong and healthy, it certainly aids the mind (mental body) when faced with a problem or disappointment. If words of negativity, hatred or hopelessness are spoken from the mental body, it can affect the physical body. If words of faith are spoken from the spiritual body and the mind (mental body) agrees with the principle, the physical body can overcome fatigue, failure, frustration, or illness more successfully.

You are a walking, talking, thinking electromagnetic force of energy. You can attract, create, speak, repel and promote conditions in your life. To discover this awareness is your journey. You can **ABUSE, DIFFUSE, MISUSE** or **USE** your personal power. You are more than your looks, status or age. The quality of your thoughts and your spiritual values are your real essence. You are what you **THINK** (mental). You are what you **BELIEVE** (spiritual). You are what you **EAT** (physical). Responsibly using your personal power can enhance every area of your life. There is a difference between ego-expansion and **SELF-REALIZATION** !

DO YOU ANSWER WHEN SPIRIT CALLS?

When we experience burn-out or desire more out of life, I believe Spirit calls us to get our attention. When we don't hear or respond... confusion and problems seem to multiply.

Remember when you were young and your mom would call your name in the neighborhood because it was getting late and you didn't have enough sense to know when it was time to come home? She was calling you home to be fed, protected nurtured, strengthened, and rest for the next day.

Sometimes Spirit calls you **IN**. Life brings illness, unwelcomed solitude, or a slow period in our lives. We perceive it to be inconvenient, painful or unfair. However, Spirit is pushing a reset button for us to go within and start over again, establish new priorities, make new choices and evaluate our strategy and patterns in life. You can go within to meditate, cry, heal, assess your life's progress and discover that sacred place where God dwells within you. With sincere effort and time, you will hear the answers you need. There you will be comforted. There you will be fed and strengthened. But you must go within when the Spirit calls. When you resist and keep looking for answers and pain killers outside your self, you miss your divine nutrients and guidance. Don't wait for God to call you **IN**. Take regular times to meditate, fast, get a massage, go on a retreat, or simply commune with nature. This will help to reduce the emergencies of illness or grief that force you to go with**IN**. Don't wait for a disappointment to make an appointment with Spirit. Is it time for you to go **IN**? Or is Spirit calling you to come **OUT**?

When Spirit calls you to come **OUT**, you may be afraid to experience more than you have in the past. When Spirit presents you with opportunities to begin again, start something new, go someplace new, do something new, or meet someone new, will you have the faith and courage? When Spirit calls you to come **OUT**, trust yourself to succeed. Come out but always know when it is time to go back **IN** to renew yourself. Trust God's presence within you for your power, provision, peace and prosperity. When it's time for you to shine, grow and prosper. Don't run out or diminish your abilities and personal power. When Spirit calls you **OUT**, be ready and confident. **GO FOR IT!** Success is a state of mind. If you believe you can, you will. If you believe you can't... you won't.

YOU ARE THE KEY

I think of myself as Robert Frost did when he stated, " I am not a teacher, but an awakener." Throughout my years of facilitating my Enlightened Circle seminars, retreats, workshops, consultations and keynote presentations, my objectives were to awaken people to their greatness and possibilities. My intention is to wake up others and myself from inaction, fear and lack of knowledge. My desire is to provide mental stimulation and a learning environment to assist participants to:

• develop courage for living
• examine the truth
• evaluate their needs
• recognize their self worth
• assume responsibility for positive change

Whether you are a student, employee, family member, team player or serving on a committee, know that you are significant to the whole. Your presence, talent and dedication to the fulfillment of a goal is valuable. You count. You are significant. Everytime you are absent or don't give your best in quality, you make a negative difference. When you give your best, you make a positive difference. I use the following example in my personal development training workshops to illustrate the importance of the individual's role in the workplace, family or team effort.

SUCCESS

Xvxn though my typxwritxr is an old modxl, it works quitx wxll xxcxpt for onx of thx kxys. I havx wishxd many timxs that it workxd pxrfxctly. It is trux that thxrx arx forty-six kxys that function wxll xnough, but just onx kxy not working makxs thx diffxrxncx.

You say to yoursxlf. "Wxll I am only onx pxrson, I won't makx or brxak thx company." But it doxs makx a diffxrxncx bxcausx to bx xfficixnt, a company, a txam, a church, a businxss and a school nxxd thx participation of xvxry pxrson.

So thx nxxt timx you find you arx only onx pxrson and you think your xfforts arx not nxxdxd, rxmxmbxr my typxwritxr and say to yoursxlf, "I am a kxy pxrson in thx company and I am nxxdxd vxry much. I do havx valux likx a diamond has valux. I am spxcial. What I do, what I say and how I participatx is important. My pxrformancx makxs a diffxrxncx!"

WHAT ARE YOU TUNED INTO?

Your faith, thoughts, words, heart intentions and actions *conduct* God's power which is transmitted through you. You are a channel, a *conduit* through which the power is conveyed. There is no power failure in God. As a conduit you can receive the wisdom, vision, guidance, protection, and strength, if you are plugged in and tuned in to the right vibration.

When you choose a frequency on the radio or TV to receive certain sounds, images, color and information, you are allowing the TV or radio to be a conduit... a channel.

You choose your thoughts, intentions, desires, motivation and words. Your conversations and what you believe indicate what vibration you are tuning into. You decide what kind of channel you will be. If you are tuned into the negative, you can't be tuned into the positive and receive the information and inspiration that positive people receive.

You can choose to be a channel for prosperity, knowledge, peace and love. You can choose to be a channel for a new car, a new home, health or more customers for your business. You can choose to be a channel for creativity and beauty. Determine what you want to focus on and stay with the vibration. The longer you stay tuned to that channel, the more you increase your chances of receiving the information and resources you need. You can't keep going back and forth on different frequencies picking up different vibrations. When you listen to the radio, do you go back and forth between channels listening to gospel, then talk radio, then rock and roll, then jazz then the news, and back and forth? When watching TV, do you constantly keep the remote control in your hand, flipping between stations with no attention span? When you are impatient and not focused, you diminish your power as a conduit in life. Your intuition, faith, and imagination make up the antenna which increases your receptivity for higher vibrations. If your spiritual antenna is not up, you will not have clear reception, only static. When you become a clear channel, you'll begin to affirm that "**I AM** a **CONDUIT** for God's power." You will begin to believe that you **CAN DO IT... because** you realize that you are a **CONDUIT.**

DO YOUR INNER WORK

As I travel, live, speak, teach and interact with so many people, I become so acutely aware of the "walking wounded." There are so many people in pain. They disguise it with smiles, clothes, cars, jewelry, homes, drinking, high risk activity, shopping, putting others down, loudness, hurting others or living in fear.

It seems that most people get their priorities out of order. They seek happiness outside of themselves. They feel that if somebody would just love them or buy them something, or if they had the right body or the right bank account, the unresolved pain within could be healed. However, these are only band-aids, and the relief is temporary.

So many are suffering from pain from their childhood, unresolved relationships, trauma or lack of genuine love in their life. One should seek to understand why they hurt, face the hurt, be courageous enough to reveal the hurt, seek healthy support to heal the hurt and then release the hurt. If the inner healing of childhood wounds, issues of abandonment, failure, sexual abuse, neglect or betrayal are resolved, that person is more likely to obtain and maintain success in their personal and professional life.

Too many times relationships, families or careers are destroyed or never realized because the inner work was never a priority until it became a glaring emergency.

I have benefited greatly from attending retreats, meditating, reading, sharing with sisterfriends, letting go and telling the truth about my inner feelings that haunted me. My progress and level of success was stunted until I was willing to remove some internal blockages. My experiences in teaching rites of passage for women and my Enlightened Circle seminars served to heal me also. It is said, "Teachers teach what they need to learn."

Give yourself the gift of "safe harbors" which are the people and environments that facilitate your healing. Create positive relationships and seek support from the "healed helpers" that can open the door. However you must walk through them.

WHO IS THE AUTHOR OF YOUR STORY?

Who has authority in your life? Who decides the quality of your life? Who determines what goals you will have? Who decides what you will eat each day? Who decides how many and what kind of relationships you will have? Who decides how much money you will earn in your life? Who decides where you will take vacations? Who decides what kind of home you will live in? Who decides what kind of car you will have? Who determines how much happiness you deserve? Who decides if you shall have peace and harmony in your life?

Your life is like a story unfolding each day. Is your life story a drama, mystery, soap opera, tragedy or comedy? The person who writes the script for your life is the "author." Either you have the <u>authority</u>, or someone else does. Writing your goals and acting upon them are ways of using your authority and personal power. Goals should be written for your personal and professional life. If you leave the quality of your life to chance or to others because you feel powerless, you are relinquishing the power, dominion and authority that the Creator granted you.

Authors use their imagination to write a story. You can use your imagination, instincts and intelligence to write your goals. As each chapter ends in your life, such as a job or a relationship, you as the author can begin to write a new chapter by writing down your goals. What do you want to happen in the next chapter of your life? What characters stay and which ones leave? Is your life one sequel after another? Do you keep repeating the same mistakes and the plot and characters never seem to change or get better?

Be the author of your life and write down your goals. Be specific about what you want. If you want more money.... how much money and when? If you want a job.... what kind, where, what benefits, what kind of boss, associates and environment do you want? If you want a new car, take time to write down the description of the car. For example, what color, year, model, stereo, CD, air conditioning, how much will the payments be, how will it feel, how many doors, sunroof, etc. If you want a new relationship, write down the values you are seeking in your mate. Today is just one page of your life, as an author you can write the script. Don't let your life be a dull book collecting dust on the shelf of life.

COPING WITH PRESSURES IN LIFE

We are spiritual beings having a human experience as a man or woman with different backgrounds. Our family background, environment, and past results shape our ability to cope and overcome misfortunes. Grief, adversity and unwelcome change are the "polishing" factors in our human development that can either make us stronger or weaker; better or bitter; positive or negative; victorious or victimized.

Just as the diamond's beauty and strength emerges from friction, cutting and polishing, we too can emerge from a layoff, illness, sluggish business, relationship "blues," car troubles or financial woes... stronger and wiser than before.

Maturing from pain teaches us that our setbacks, disappointments and seeming obstacles can be perceived as blessings and/or lessons. If one resists, complains and perpetuates their pain, they perceive themselves as helpless and powerless victims. A person who is spiritually grounded, surrounded with loving relationships, goal oriented and lives in a nurturing environment is more likely to cope with stress in a positive way.

When "shift" happens... do you run to food, drugs, TV, sleep, alcohol, sex, the mall, gossiping, fighting/hurting others and other self destructive behavior? These are negative coping mechanisms which are "Temporary pain relievers" that can only lead to disaster and defeat.

Positive alternatives for coping with stress are physical exercise; mediation/prayer; a long bath; a retreat; writing in your journal; change of daily routine; reading or music; fasting; let go of toxic relationships; seeking counsel and/or support group.

Learn how to become decisive and take action instead of being overwhelmed with fear or anxiety. Fear freezes you. Action will free you up.

NEGATIVE STRESS vs. POSITIVE STRESS

Reality is subject to change without notice. Loss of jobs, ending relationships, earthquakes, fires, floods, financial setback or ill health can happen at any time without notice. If you can cope with stress in a positive way, your chances of survival are greater. Life will challenge you sooner or later with the lesson of "letting go." If you can't pass the test, your suffering is prolonged.

Feeling that your decisions and choices are useless is negative stress. When you are overwhelmed, feeling powerless and perceive that your future is beyond your control, this is negative stress.

Rising to the challenge, feeling confident and a sense of control over your destiny is positive stress. Being aware of your possibilities, options and ability to make things happen with the power of thought, words and actions is healthy.

Here are some suggested affirmations for change and letting go of the familiar when experiencing unexpected or unwelcomed change:

I trust that change brings good things.
I am a student of change.
I surrender to the flow of change.
I am capable to make new decisions.
I let go of resistance.
I am proactive vs. reactive in the midst of change.
I trust myself to adjust to change.
I am learning to adjust to new environments.
I am willing to surrender my comfort zone.
I am willing to explore new options.
I am willing to let go of the familiar.
I embrace new adventures.
I can overcome anxiety about change.
I am safe and secure.
I accept my feelings.
I will identify my resources and abilities.
I am willing to be responsible for my future.
I can start now taking steps to get what I want.
I'm always in the right place,
at the right time
and prepared.

SUCCESS AND SURVIVAL

Success and survival are a daily choice. Some people are "destined" to be successful, but most of us have to be "determined" to be successful.

What does success look like and feel like for you? Have you redefined your personal and professional goals?

Don't live your life by chance. Your choices clearly stated, written down, meditated upon and acted upon can create a rewarding and fulfilling life-style for you.

Everyday you need to recommit to your goals. Everyday you must decide if you will just "get through" the day or "get something from the day." Unless you specifically plan a day of mental and physical rest, any day that isn't productive is a wasted day.

Time is precious. Every day is a special occasion. So don't put off any longer doing the activities that bring you closer to inner peace, prosperity, health, loving relationships, realization of your goals and daily joy.

Striving and arriving at your success destination require self-discipline, commitment, quality, and hard work. Maintaining your success requires even more self-discipline, commitment, quality and hard work. Everyday make a conscious choice of what you want to welcome and keep in your life. Your attitude and agenda for each day determines what you will ultimately achieve and receive.

Yesterday is history. Tomorrow is a mystery. Today is a gift called the "present." This day choose right action, right thoughts and right beliefs to succeed and survive.

PLUGGED IN AND CORDLESS

All my life I used telephones that confined me to one room. I can remember my first experiences with a cordless phone in my home. I would sit still at my desk or sit still on the couch using the cordless phone. It finally dawned on me that I didn't have to stay in one room. I was free to wash dishes while using the phone. I was free to walk from one room to another looking for a file in my office or unload the clothes in the washing machine. I could stand outside talking to a neighbor and not miss a call.

Options, freedom, no cords, nothing stopping me from moving around was a new way of communication. So why did I continue to limit myself when I first installed the phone? The answer is **conditioning**. The old way of doing something became a limiting habit. Even though nothing was stopping me from moving around, my subconscious still limited me to a small area. Only through self-observation and continued use of the cordless phone was I able to break the old habit of limitation.

Like our ancestors who were conditioned to be slaves and limited in their mobility, thinking and believing, it takes time to adjust to the new reality when someone tells you that you are free. A new world of choices, options and selections can be confusing, frightening and unbelievable.

If you are convinced you are powerless and limited, your behavior will reflect that concept. When you become a seeker of knowledge and pursue higher living, you will begin to form new habits. You will discover that only you and your beliefs have stopped you in the past from growing. You will discover that an invisible cord links you to a Higher Power. Only you can disconnect yourself. There is no power shortage in God. You are given power, volition, choices, dominion and authority over your life. You are free to choose what you think, what you believe and how you will behave. Your habits, memories, knowledge and experience are the sum total of you.

Have a sense of humor. I used to laugh at myself when I realized I was limiting myself with the cordless phone. I was willing to self-correct. Remember, as long as you recharge your life spiritually, physically and mentally, you are plugged into the Power even though you don't see the cord. Don't limit yourself, success awaits you!

PROBLEMS OR PEARLS?

My Father was a jeweler in Washington D.C. where I was born. When he passed, I kept some of his books on gemology from his store. I read about the story of pearls, especially the black pearls, one of the most valuable gems.

Most gems are minerals formed over thousands of years beneath Mother Earth. Pearls, however, are born inside the shells of oysters beneath the sea. When a foreign substance like a grain of sand or a parasite enters the shell, the oyster produces and covers the irritation with circular layers of a solution called "nacre." After 7 years of this process of layering, divers bring up the beautiful pearl that emerges from the darkness. The divers sell the pearls that only exist because of the initial intrusion and process that follows.

Can you understand the wonderful lesson the pearl teaches us? When an unwelcome irritation, event or circumstance enters our world, we can cover our irritation with a solution too. We can turn our problems into pearls. We can learn from the unwelcome pain, setback or problem. All challenges are temporary. Some are for a few minutes, a few days or a few years. When it's all over, there's a valuable lesson to be learned.

As I recalled my own personal challenges and talked to over-comers across the nation in my travels, I collected many pearls. Some of the best poems, books, songs, art, inventions or social changes have been created from experiences of pain or inconvenience. People have started their own businesses after being laid off jobs. Illness motivated others to adopt a healthier lifestyle. After recovering from the grief of losing a loved one, people have become dedicated to living a more meaningful life. Others have learned lessons in self-esteem and self-love when a relationship ended.

Stories of action, creativity, faith and endurance are testimonies to the lesson of the pearl. When a problem occurs, you can choose to surround the condition with negative feelings of shame or blame. Or you can choose action and the right attitude to transform the irritation. Each time you learned a lesson and passed the test of pain, you gained a precious pearl. If you ever turned a potentially negative situation into a positive one, you gained a pearl. Learn to value your experience and your "pearls of wisdom."

THE GREATEST "WAIT LOSS" PROGRAM

Procrastination is a thief. You wait... you lose. You can lose money, ideas, health, family, friends, customers, self-esteem and peace of mind. Procrastination promotes hesitation, isolation, desperation, perspiration and frustration. The robbers and thieves of delay that can steal from you are:

•doubt	•lack of information
•anger	•lack of planning
•fear	•laziness
•lack of action	•low self-esteem

To overcome procrastination, one must seek progress over perfection. If you are waiting for all conditions to be just right, you'll never get started. To waste time is to waste your life. To master your time... is to master your life. Time is more precious than diamonds. Today is a **gift**. That is why it is called the **present**. Your power and potential for a brighter future are in the present moment and what you do with it. Open up the gift, use it. Don't wait for a special occasion. Every day is a special occasion! What are you waiting for? Small changes daily can bring about a BIG change in your life. You can do something right now, today, that would take you one step closer to realizing your goal.

We measure time in minutes, hours, months and years. The clock tells us when to get up, go to work, when to eat and when to go to bed. We tell time by calenders, clocks, candles and celebrations. Some people kill time, some call time, some beat time, some waste time and some try to turn back time. It is **irreversible** and **irreplaceable**. We can't manage time. But we can have **respect** for it and manage what we do with time.

Sometimes the greatest stumbling blocks to our growth are **EGO** and **FEAR**. Once you conquer and arrest these thieves, you will no longer be stuck in a pattern of inaction. These two thieves still your ability to grow. If you can go to sleep each night knowing you have made progress that day, your rest is peaceful and you wake the next day ready to continue.

On the following pages, I submit to you some reasons why we procrastinate, steps to overcome waiting, an action list, and a poem on page 98 I wrote after my painful lesson in waiting and losing.

REASONS WHY PEOPLE PROCRASTINATE

1. **DESIRE PERFECTION**

   "I want to wait until I have enough money or lose weight."

   "I'll wait until everybody approves and believes in me."

   "I'll wait until I'm perfect and know everything."

2. **FEAR OF MAKING A MISTAKE**

   "If I fail, I will look so stupid."

   "I want guarantees. I want to be sure."

   "I "know-it-all". My image and ego are important."

3. **FEAR OF RESPONSIBILITY**

   "I don't know **what** to do".

   "I don't know **how** to do it."

   "Why can't someone else do it for me."

   "I'm afraid I'll mess it up."

   "It's too hard making decisions. I'm a victim."

4. **NO GOALS - NO PLAN**

   "Whatever happens, happens."

   "I'm not sure what I want."

   "I'll just wait and see."

5. **LACK OF FAITH, SELF-DOUBT, LOW SELF-ESTEEM**

   "Maybe it won't work, so why try."

   "God doesn't hear my prayers. I'm not worthy."

   "I don't think I can do it, I'm not smart/pretty/rich enough."

6. **LACK OF INFORMATION**

   "I don't know anybody who can help."

   "I don't have time to read or take a class."

7. WRONG ASSOCIATIONS/RELATIONSHIPS
   "He/she won't go with me."
   "He/she won't let me."
   "He/she doesn't believe in me."
   "No one I know has been successful."

8. RELIANCE ON OTHERS TO ACT OR DECIDE
   FOR YOU
   "I thought he/she was taking care of it."
   "I've never done that before, can you do it for me?"
   "I don't trust myself, what do you think?"

9. TRAPPED IN A COMFORT ZONE
   "It's not that bad, I'm used to it."

10. FEAR OF THE UNKNOWN
    "I don't know what to expect. I like being in
    control."

11. PERCEIVE CONFLICT AS PAINFUL - DON'T WANT
    TO "ROCK THE BOAT"
    "Everytime I try something new, I am attacked or
    questioned. Keeping everybody else happy and
    not angry at me is more important. I'll postpone
    my happiness rather than cope with change,
    resistance or challenges."

HOW TO OVERCOME PROCRASTINATION

1. **DON'T SPEND MAJOR TIME WITH MINOR PEOPLE**
   People that are negative, pessimistic, waste time and involved in self-destructive behavior will have a negative influence on you. People that are on-the-grow, active, productive, open to change, spiritual, caring and optimistic are contagious. Their attitudes and habits can influence you in a positive way.

2. **DON'T SPEND MAJOR TIME ON MINOR THINGS**
   Don't confuse activity with accomplishments. Sometimes we engage in distracting and insignificant activities to avoid action on what is really important.

3. **IDENTIFY YOUR TIME WASTERS**
   Do you watch too much television, sleep too much, gossip too much, eat too much, party too much? Don't just "get through" the day, "get more" from your day!

4. **REWARD YOURSELF WHEN A GOAL IS COMPLETED**
   For example, I make agreements with myself that if I complete certain paperwork or successfully reach a personal goal about food, I can buy a new pair of shoes or go to the Marina for a walk to relax and meditate.

5. **TACKLE THE TOUGHEST TASK FIRST**
   Avoiding a big task steals your energy and effectiveness in performance. Free yourself up. Do the hardest thing first so you can enjoy the rest of the day.

6. **DELEGATE SOME TASKS TO OTHERS, DON'T TRY TO DO EVERYTHING**
   Don't be afraid to ask for help. Retire your superwoman/man cape.

7. **LEARN WHAT SORT OF ATMOSPHERE YOU WORK BEST IN**
   I found that I get more work done in a clean, orderly and pleasant room of fresh air, open windows, soft music, a comfortable chair, and pleasant people around.

"GET IT DONE" Checklist

___ car repair
___ homework
___ family reunion
___ visit a friend
___ church
___ exercise class
___ diet
___ new home
___ new car
___ family meeting
___ new wardrobe
___ repay loans
___ reading
___ taxes
___ job interview
___ update goals
___ travel
___ go to library
___ begin hobby
___ take a test
___ creative writing
___ say "I'm sorry"
___ say "I love you"
___ say "I need help"
___ attend a meeting
___ buy furniture
___ quit a job/project
___ research
___ spiritual faith
___ quality time with loved one

___ doctor visit
___ car registration
___ voter registration
___ school registration
___ vacation
___ stop smoking
___ stop drug abuse
___ new relationship
___ savings/investment
___ home improvement
___ business start up
___ return phone calls
___ new customers
___ buy office equipment
___ meditation/quiet time
___ better spending habits
___ credit card spending
___ return borrowed item
___ begin project
___ parent involvement
___ entertainment
___ clean up work area
___ clean up closets
___ clean up car
___ attend a conference
___ renew friendship
___ paperwork
___ control emotions of
fear, anger, worry
___ attend class/seminar

STAY IN THE LIGHT

My signature statement for years now has been, "Stay in the Light," because I have experienced pain, anger and loss. It seemed like the darkness would never end. My personal affirmation reminded me that I had a choice of light or darkness.

When you toss and turn all night about bills, about your children, from illness or grief, it seems like the sun will never rise again. Actually the sun doesn't rise. The earth turns to the sun.

When we are experiencing our "40 days and 40 nights" of despair, we have to turn to the Light. Just as the earth turns away from the sun, it eventually rotates back to reflect light where there was once darkness.

When you are in between jobs, without transportation, without love or without money, affirm that it is temporary. This attitude shifts your thinking to hope, optimism, positive outcomes and action. This attitude helps you to shed light on the problem that needs to be solved. The light helps you to see possibilities you couldn't see in darkness.

The darkness of pain, anger, jealousy or no faith can blind you from seeing and believing there are solutions available. When you walk into a dark room, you're more likely to stub your toe on the furniture or fall. You can't find a door for escape. You can't see the windows to open. You don't see a clear path. However, when you turn the LIGHT ON, you can SEE.

If you cannot see the possibilities, options and a way out, you need to find the light switch. Turn on your faith. Connect with God's power. Meditating, praying and a life of love, service and forgiveness are how you keep your "light bill paid." To avoid a power shortage or darkness, keep your power on. When faced with a challenge, you will have the faith to stay in the light to find solutions.

Try the positive habit of telling others to "stay in the light" when you see them struggling with a problem. Be encouraging. Your encouragement is helpful to someone lost in the darkness. It can help them find their own "light switch."

AROUND EVERY FLOWERING TREE ARE INSECTS
(African Proverb)

When a flower opens up to realize it's potential of beauty, color and fragrance, the insects are attracted and begin to buzz around and eat away at the new flower.

When you open up to new places, people and ideas... you will begin your evolution toward self-realization. When you want more out of life than your school friends, co-workers, family, peers or those choosing a lower standard of living, don't be surprised or discouraged when the "insects" come. They will say:

> "Why do you want to go there?"
> "Why do want to be with that person?"
> "You can't make any money doing that."
> "Why don't you hang out with us anymore?"
> "Oh, a little bit of (drugs, alcohol, cake) won't hurt you."
> "Oh, you think you're better than us."
> "Why don't you stay with this "secure" job? Why give it up for your own business, which will probably fail?"
> "If you travel that far, something bad may happen."
> "That idea will never work."

When you desire to grow and change, it forces those around you to look at themselves in the mirror. It may be painful for them to realize that they need to change and work on their own life improvement.

Success requires taking calculated risks vs. dumb chances. Someone wise once said, "If you want to steal second base, you have to leave first base." Be willing to distance yourself or let go of people draining you of enthusiasm and self-esteem. Believe in yourself and continue with positive action. New people and support from unexpected channels will begin to show up in your life to reward your consistent efforts toward your worthy goal.

It's nature's law for insects to gather around a flowering tree. It's not unusual for people uninformed, fearful or negative to question someone who is more positive or different than them. Be aware. You can <u>expect</u> it... but you don't have to <u>accept</u> it. Don't let their fears and words stop your personal or professional growth. There are people who will appreciate the beauty you bring to the "flower garden of life." So go ahead and **BLOOM**!

ATTRACTION POWER

The way you express yourself with thoughts, intentions, beliefs and actions is energy radiating from you called "attraction power." Understanding how to use your "attraction power" is NOT just for attracting your ideal mate. You can attract success, customers, friends, resources, ideas, opportunities, a new home, car, travel, harmony, mentors, scholarships, loans, books, referrals and money.

The echo of our ancestors reminds us to "know thyself." The knowledge of self activates your attraction power. Through study, observation and experience you will discover how powerful your words, your expectations, your giving and body language attract certain people and circumstances. Your invisible internal thoughts and hopes of yesterday will become visible today or tomorrow according to your concentration and use of your personal power. Your dominate thought becomes your destiny.

The right foods in your body increases your attraction power. Healthy foods increase your stamina, energy and give you a radiant glow. A life-style of exercise, fruits, vegetables and water affect your cell regeneration thus enhancing the vibrations you emit. A healthy body is resilient and insulated from stress. Your healthy body can become a **magnetiz**ing force in the home, workplace and the world to draw to you what you **energize** with your thoughts, words and actions.

Self-esteem and knowledge radiate your attraction power. These qualities draw people to you who wouldn't, under other circumstances, offer you help and/or information.

The positive healthy mind is tuned into a higher frequency and reality which offers ideas and a life force not experienced by those who are toxic and tired. Positive right thinking creates and believes on a higher plane. Like will attract like. You'll begin to meet people who think like you. You will attract people and experiences that reflect your level of thinking and living.

Don't be surprised when good things happen to you. Don't say, "I can't believe it!" when doors of opportunity open for you. When people and circumstances seem to be there just when you needed it, know that it's the "law of attraction" working in you and for you. Use the power wisely!

HEALTH IS WEALTH

Your body houses your mind and spirit. Respect, love and nurture your body with healthy foods and healthy thoughts. Certain foods and negative thoughts can be toxic. They both create dis-ease in your body and life conditions. You cannot perform and use your talents in life when your body is toxic, tired, stressed, depressed, sick and overweight. Take time to assess your eating habits, how you cope with stress, your sexual life-style, emotions and time management. Too often the emphasis is to alter the outward appearance with cosmetics, clothes, plastic surgery, hair, or jewelry in order to cover up our emptiness and darkness inside. Work from the inside out to transform your external beauty. Your attraction power shines brighter from within.

Health is your first wealth. Reviewing and taking action where necessary in regards to your health patterns, as listed below, can produce the energy, enthusiasm and stamina required to pursue your goals and dreams. If you want to be alert, active, spiritually strong, creative and have a clear mind in times of crisis, review this checklist.

- smoking	- breathing exercises
- alcohol	- sense of humor
- drugs	- massage
- stress	- negative thinking
- meat	- sexual lifestyle
- exercise	- rest
- fresh air	- vitamins/herbal intake
- sugar	- recreational activities
- white flour	- fruits/vegetables
- water intake	- medical checkups

I learned the painful way from fibroid tumors and painful monthly menstrual cycles how to value my health. My mother's passing from breast cancer and a family history of asthma prompted me to become educated about correct eating habits and natural herbal supplements. I learned that the reduction and eventual elimination of red meats and sugar will reduce the tumors and very painful monthly cramps. I have enjoyed weight reduction, increased energy and reduced pain from cramps with herbal tablets of red raspberry, aloe vera, cascara sagrada, goldenseal & more. The American diet has too much sugar and chemicals and not enough "live" food, vitamins and minerals which the body needs to regenerate itself. You can educate yourself and your family to maintain proper health.

COMFORT ZONE

There are people who love dogs and cats. For some reason I love ducks. For years I collected pictures, pot holders, towels, place mats... anything with ducks. About 4 years ago, I took it one step further. I bought 4 beautiful ducks for my back yard to enjoy. Of course, my sons thought I was strange, and that their friends were "normal" because they had dogs or cats, not ducks.

When I first brought them home, they would QUACK, QUACK, QUACK very loudly in protest. When my sons took out the trash and left the gate open, my ducks would escape and I would laugh watching my sons chase the ducks down the street to bring them back to their new home.

Years have passed now, I only have 2 ducks left. My sons or the gardener occasionally leave the gate open. But a strange thing has happened. My ducks don't try to leave anymore. "Lady" and "JP" don't quack very much anymore, only if they are hungry. They don't spread their wings. They are very complacent and comfortable. If they were around other ducks, they would realize that they could fly. They don't have to remain in my confined backyard. They don't try to escape to a new world when opportunity opens the gate.

Are you like my ducks? Have you forgotten to (quack) speak up and protest a negative condition in your life? Have you settled for limitations or less? If you don't spend time with people who spread their wings, create, produce, act, change, grow and expand their horizons... then you won't believe it is possible for you to fly. Who clipped your wings? Are you afraid to leave a negative or toxic relationship? Are you afraid to fail or succeed in a new city, new career, new relationship?

If you don't change or grow, you'll find yourself in a rut, a comfort zone. Fear "freezes" you. You become paralyzed and never realize what life has to offer. Action is the cure. Action will "free" you up. Life does require courage and faith. My ducks continue to teach me a very valuable lesson... life is meant to be lived, explored, and enjoyed. Learn from my ducks. Don't limit yourself. Liberate yourself!

SHIFT HAPPENS

Even though change is uncomfortable or frightening, the more you resist, the more it will persist. Learning to surrender and yield to shifts in careers, relationships and external conditions that you have no control of can reduce your stress. It may seem like your life is "falling apart" at times, but it may be "coming together" in a better way.

Change means exchange. Instead of saying you have been laid off a job... say your career path has been redirected. You will be exchanging one career path for another. As hard as it is to let go of relationships, you will maintain self-esteem and serenity if you perceive the shift as making room for a better relationship. Sometimes when your ego or fear stops you from making a necessary change, shift happens and creates the change that you were trying to avoid. Life will <u>invite you</u> or <u>challenge you</u> to grow and shine.

Shift will demand you grow and stretch in your faith and courage. Don't get caught up labeling the shift as "bad" or "good." It just IS. In time, it will all make sense if you affirm that divine order is always taking place in your life. It's easy to affirm this when all is well. The true test comes in times of unwelcome and unexpected change. This is when your level of faith will help you to trust and keep pressing forward even when you're not sure what to expect next.

Change is a part of life. The seasons change. The economy changes. People and circumstances are unpredictable. Children, parents and you will grow older. Mother nature cleanses, shakes, erupts and burns. But new life always returns and restores in time.

If you greet the shifts in your life with negative and fearful emotions, the shift will seem like a revolution. If you greet the shifts in your life with a positive and hopeful attitude, the shifts in your life can be perceived as evolution. Chaos could mean a time of creativity. Something is trying to be born.

How do you perceive the changes in your life? Do you feel like a helpless victim? Or do you accept that shift happens in everyone's life? If you take it personal and feel that life is against you, you have given your power away. Don't doubt your power to endure and overcome adversity. No one is immune from pain or grief. You can successfully recover from the shift in your life... depending on your attitude.

KISS MY POSITIVE ATTITUDE

In living your purpose and passion, there may be family, friends or society who will misjudge you. When you live your life with purpose, enthusiasm and commitment, it becomes a part of you. To others <u>without</u> a purpose, you may seem strange or selfish. It's difficult for them to share in your vision and eternal optimism. Remember that saying, "Misery loves company?" Their psychological abuse, unworthiness or unhappiness can be toxic and affect you. Because they don't know their purpose or passion in life, it makes them restless, negative, and lack that spark in their lives. They may try to block your happiness or keep you on their level of unfulfillment. Your conversations, smile, activities and new found energy may be disturbing to the one who has no energy, no vision, and no self esteem.

Knowing your purpose in life can lengthen your life and enrich your livingness in spite of challenges. Your disposition becomes positive and pleasant because you have something to live for. When others want to stomp on your dreams and tell you that you can't or shouldn't, your response can be "kiss my positive attitude." You can also tell them..."thanks for sharing, I respect your opinions, so please respect mine. I know who I AM and what I must do. My living must not be in vain."

Being responsible in life means, "responding to your ability." You have the ability to create happiness or havoc. You have the ability to create success or stress. You have the ability to choose miracles or misery. You have the choice and ability to respond negatively or positively to conditions in your life. An enlightened person responds to his ability in how he thinks, forgives, creates, plans, speaks, prays, reacts, acts, serves, dreams and actualizes.

Once you own, celebrate and act upon your purpose in life, you accept your responsibility to live your life to the fullest. You rise above limited living and thinking. You take responsibility for the quality of your life. Some people have not taken responsibility for the quality of their lives. They still operate from blame, shame, false pride, fear, anger, ignorance or doubt. The best way you can inspire them is to live your life doing and giving your best. Be true to your purpose in life whether it is being a teacher, healer, salesperson, technician, visionary, entrepreneur, painter, dancer, writer, volunteer, traveler, student, parent, comedian, clerk, banker or football player.

OBEDIENCE TO YOUR PURPOSE

I think one of the greatest fears is the fear that your life has no purpose. You are here for a reason. Your life has meaning. Find it. Embrace it. Honor it. Enjoy it..

"Obedience to his genius is the only liberating influence."
Emerson

You will begin to listen to yourself and God's plan for your life when you realize other people's answers do NOT work for you. The word of God always whispers to the willing mind. Once you discover your dream and purpose in life, it is difficult and painful to do anything else. Once you embrace your purpose, the Lord will add the thread to the web you have begun. You just have to get started. The hardest thing you ever do, may be the greatest thing you ever do.

"Make yourself necessary to the world, and mankind
will give you bread."
Emerson

The seven (7) spiritual requirements for effective living are 1) positive attitude; 2) quiet centering; 3) consciousness of God; 4) love; 5) dedication to purpose; 6) forgiveness; 7) service.

How Do I Measure Success - By Ralph Waldo Emerson
To laugh often and love much
to win the respect of intelligent people
and the affection of children
to earn the appreciation of honest critics
and to endure the betrayal of false friends,
to appreciate beauty,
to find the best in others,
to give of one's self,
to leave the world a bit better,
whether by a healthy child,
a garden patch,
or a redeemed social condition,
to have played and laughed
with enthusiasm and sung exultation;
to know that even ONE life has breathed
easier because you have lived.
This is to have succeeded.

KNOWLEDGE IS ECSTASY

The renowned scientist, writer, and professor of astronomy and space sciences, Carl Sagan, has a insatiable curiosity about how the universe works. In his studies, he states that we human beings are an intelligent species, and that when we use our intelligence properly, it gives us pleasure. "Understanding is a kind of ecstasy," he states. I agree.

Those who are hungry for knowledge, answers, solutions and understanding of the why, what, who, where and when, are excited and highly stimulated by the discovery of truth.

People who turn over every stone don't take "no" for an answer, and persevere are worthy of study. One who is determined to gain knowledge and overcome ignorance and/or obstacles becomes a visionary, an innovator, and a leader. They are worthy of honor.

Frederick Douglass, born in slavery escaped and became a freedom fighter for slaves, a newspaper editor, a lecturer, an author and a U.S. Minister to Haiti. However, Frederick Douglass had to fight and persevere in his pursuit for knowledge to learn how to read and write. His master would not allow him to read, or write, or become educated.

As a young boy, Frederick would take bread from the master's house when he would go on errands. He would use the bread to bribe the young white children he played with to teach him how to read and write. Frederick was hungry for knowledge. He was curious and determined. He was willing to do whatever it took to be educated and liberated. His knowledge and understanding became his ecstasy. Learning how to read and write stimulated him and made him feel confident and strong. The deep well of mental darkness he once lived now had a ladder of escape. His ladder to the light of freedom, self-esteem and a purpose in life was his new found and paid for knowledge. People tried to stop him. People tried to make him feel inferior and unworthy. It was difficult to endure, but he was determined to learn and overcome the "physical and mental chains" that kept him enslaved. His intelligence gave pleasure, which, in turn, assisted others in their escape to freedom. The "bread of knowledge" that fed and sustained him was literally paid for with the bread that was stolen. But his dignity and rights were stolen. It was risky and forbidden to take the bread, but he didn't allow any one or any thing to stop him from reaching his goal.

BE A GOOD MANAGER

The word "manage" originates from the Latin word "manus" which means "hand." "Manage" means to control, handle, govern, direct, train, influence, and to take responsibility.

Your personal success is determined by how well you "manage" your life, emotions, money, talent, time, and relationships. It is in your "hands" how you "manage" your **TIME, TALENT,** and **TREASURES**.

TIME is a precious commodity:
- Plan your day, have an agenda, create a list of things to do.
- Have someone or an answering service screen your telephone calls.
- Don't waste your time with time wasters i.e., TV, negative people, gossiping, too much sleep, activities, meetings or organizations that don't contribute to your growth.
- Ask questions to avoid making mistakes that cause you to repeat a task the second time.
- Time is money. Respect schedules, deadlines & appointments. Keep your commitments.

TALENT - what you don't use, you lose:
- You have a God given ability or talent that can be developed. Give your gift to the world. We're waiting!
- Sharpen your skills and talents. Read, take classes and network.
- Turn your passion into a profession. People will pay for your talent or service if they see value
- Don't underestimate your abilities. Find a need, and fill it.. Recognize and honor your self-worth. There is something unique within you!

TREASURES
- Your family, health, friends, home, collections, business, material possessions, monetary wealth, ideas and your imagination are your treasures.
- Don't spend so much time earning your "salt" that you forget your "sugar." Seek balance.
- Protect your health, eat properly and exercise.
- Avoid stress, and have a positive attitude, have positive outlets for emotional support.
- Become a wise money manager. Increase your knowledge about economics, savings, and investing. Increase your earning potential.
- Don't hesitate to show appreciation and love.
- Have an attitude of gratitude, and acknowledge God for all your blessings, big or small.

THE POWER OF IDEAS

An acorn is complete just being an acorn, but it is not "fulfilled" until it reaches its potential. A thousand forests are in one acorn. The potential, the seeds, the blueprint for more forests lie within the acorn. You are complete as you are. But are you fulfilled? Are you reaching your potential? Ideas in you are waiting to be realized.

John Roebling was an engineer with an idea. His idea was to bridge over the river tying Manhattan Island with Brooklyn in New York. It was a daring idea, but all the bridge building experts and structural engineers said it was "impossible." Some agreed that the river might be spanned, but that a 1,595 foot span would never stand up against the winds and the tides. However, John Roebling and his son Washington, figured out how the problems could be solved and how the obstacles would be overcome.

As construction began, John Roebling was killed on the job. In the same accident, his son Washington suffered the bends underneath the water. The son survived, but was left with permanent brain damage, causing him to never walk or talk again. Everybody said, "Give up... forget the project." But not Washington. He developed a code of communication by touching one finger to the arm of his wife. He communicated the dream through his wife to the engineers on the project.

For 13 years, Washington Roebling supervised construction of the bridge. Finally in 1883, traffic streamed across the completed Brooklyn Bridge. When Washington Roebling was told the news, he wept with joy. The impossible dream became a reality. It was the largest suspension bridge in the world when it was completed. It was hailed the "8th Wonder of the World."

He did not give up because of what others said or the incredible obstacles and odds he faced.

WHO or WHAT is stopping you? What you start building now may not be finished by you, but the next generation of visionaries can continue your dream. Ego, pride, fear, setbacks and limited thinking are failure's favorite tools. The tools of success are commitment, perseverance, team effort, imagination and vision to see what others can't see. Ordinary people can do **EXTRA** ordinary things.

ENTREPRENEUR STEPS FOR SUCCESS

ADVERTISE your product or service. Everyone recognizes the golden arches. It symbolizes a household name. McDonalds, a successful hamburger franchise around the world, STILL advertises aggressively. It maximizes its advertising potential.

Don't underestimate the power of advertisement in the media for your product or service. Make sure your business allocates enough dollars for advertising.

Choose the best advertising medium for your product or service. Will newspaper, souvenir booklets, telecommunications, radio or TV best market your business? If you don't advertise, it's like business suicide!

BELIEVE in your product or service. Your chances of success are greater if you really believe in and love what you do. When the growing pains come, unexpected setbacks, and customers slack off, you will need the staying power and determination to overcome. It's easy to abandon ship if you don't really believe in or love what you're doing.

CUSTOMER SERVICE is essential to the survival of your business. Train your team for quality, dependability, customer anticipation, customer satisfaction, people skills, follow through, a pleasant attitude and courtesy. Good news about your business will travel fast... but bad news travels even faster. People tend to have a long memory when it comes to negative experiences with a waiter or sales person.

DARE to be different. Creativity can be the difference in business profits and success. What ordinary thing can you create in an extraordinary way? If competition does it small, can you do it bigger? If competition does it bigger, can you make it smaller? What about convenience? Brainstorm with your family, staff or a total stranger. Ask questions. Don't do the same thing year after year. What can you rearrange? What can you get rid of? Do you think locally or globally? Put yourself in your customer's shoes. Would you spend money on your product or service? Why would you return? It takes just a little extra effort to be above average.

ENTHUSIASM is contagious and can positively affect your business associates and customers. Stay motivated!

NETWORKING WORKS!

If you want to go further in life, networking is the vehicle to take you there. Networking is the answer for:

- looking for a new job
- wanting more customers for your business
- looking for a new home
- looking for a business loan/grant
- looking for a scholarship for your child
- seeking creative ideas
- seeking active/productive people
- updating yourself on current events in your community
- needing a new car

Networking connects you with an information loop connected to other loops of information. We live in the "information age." Networking keeps you informed on the important HOW, WHO, WHAT and WHERE. People are more likely to help you, or do business with you if they meet you in person or share something in common with you.

Networking is an art. Learn how to be personable and confident. Distribute your business cards. Ask questions. Introduce yourself to new people. Associate with new organizations. Read your local newspaper. Meet your Chamber of Commerce. Know the staff at your school. Make yourself known to your bank manager. Meet the decision makers, presidents, CEOs, board of directors, entrepreneurs and community activists. Be open to new places and people.

Networking works... **if you work it**. If you plant your seeds (business cards, thank you notes, participate in activities, show up at meetings, volunteer, write articles)... your seeds will eventually produce opportunities. Don't get discouraged easily. As a professional speaker, I have received many invitations to speak to organizations 3 or 4 years after I passed out business cards, made a phone call or attended a conference/meeting.

Take time to develop professional relationships and develop yourself. People may not need your product or service today. However, if you leave a <u>Positive</u> impression... <u>Persistence, P</u>rofessionalism and <u>Patience</u> can <u>Pay</u> off.

FOUR ANSWERS

As a parent, I've learned that I couldn't always tell my sons "yes" to their every need. I came to realize that in order to really empower my sons and to do what was best for their higher good, there were four different answers I could give when they wanted something. Also, in my spiritual and emotional maturity, I learned that my spiritual parent, God, wants the same for me. I, too, had to learn to hear and adhere to four different answers.

You may be like a lot of sincere people who pray, serve, sacrifice and believe strongly in what you ask. You may experience frustration, feeling your questions or prayers are not answered. If you don't recognize the four different ways that life will respond to your questions, prayers and desires, you may stop asking and praying. You may continually grow impatient, weary and even lose your faith.

God's silent intelligence answers us. However, our ego, anger, impatience or lack of knowledge keeps us from hearing the answers, or we hear the answers and don't like it. Think now of one of your earnest goals or desires. Honestly ask yourself if your answer is:

SLOW - You're moving too fast. You're not old enough. You're not ready. Slow down you're trying to do too much. Slow down and focus on details and quality. Accept divine order and trust. Study nature's pace and remember the process of planting seeds, nurturing the seed and allowing the seed to come forth when it is ready. Patience needs to be developed.

GROW - Take time to learn more about life. Learn more about your business. Learn more about yourself. Learn more about the relationship you are contemplating. Grow in disciplining your emotions, time, money, eating habits. Grow in integrity. Grow in faith. Enhance your education. Improve your skills. Polish up your talents. Grow in overcoming addictions or obsessions. Learn forgiveness. Grow in your capacity to love.

NO - It's not appropriate at this time. It's not for the highest good of ALL concerned. It's not for your best interest. There is something or someone better if you're willing to let go.

GO - Door of opportunity closes quickly. Don't hesitate. Have courage. The answer is yes. Be responsible. Be thankful.

PARENTING SUCCESS

"I had the meanest mother in the world. While other kids had candy for breakfast, I had to eat cereal, eggs and toast. While other children had cokes and candy for lunch, I had a sandwich. As you can guess, my dinner was different from other kids' dinners, too.

My Mother insisted on knowing where we were at all times. You'd think we were on a chain gang or something. She had to know who our friends were and what we were doing.

I am ashamed to admit it, but she actually had the nerve to break the child labor law. She made us work. We had to wash dishes, make the beds and learn how to cook. That woman must have stayed awake nights thinking up things for us kids to do. And she always insisted that we tell the truth, the whole truth, and nothing but the truth.

By the time we were teenagers, she was much wiser and our life became even more unbearable. None of this tooting the car horn for us to come running; she embarrassed us to no end by insisting that the boys come to the door to get us.

I forgot to mention that most of our friends were allowed to date at the mature age of 12 and 13, but our old-fashioned Mother refused to let us date until we were 15. She really raised a bunch of "squares." None of us was ever arrested for shoplifting or busted for drugs. And who do we have to thank for this? You're right, our mean Mother.

I am trying to raise my children to stand a little straighter and taller and I am secretly tickled to pieces when my children call me mean. I thank God for giving me the meanest Mother in the world."

(sent to Ann Landers reprinted in Oakland Tribune 1977)

I could have been the author of this letter, thanks to my Mother and Aunt Janet. And, I'm sure my sons (John & Jason) felt their father and I have been mean at times. I strongly believe that as parents, we should not try to be popular with our kids to win their favor. Your children lose in life when you lower your expectations, values and guidance. Love and appropriate rules provide your child with a sense of security and belonging.

So parents don't get discouraged when your children display resentment and resistance to your loving guidance. Don't give up. It's normal for youth to try to test their limits. Draw your **boundaries**, build **bridges** of communication and hold true to your **beliefs**. One day they will thank you for showing the love that so many children have never received.

YOUR GOALS ARE YOUR CHILDREN

I have discovered as many similarities in developing my goals as I have in developing my two sons. Similar to a goal, a child is born from a seed planted in the womb. While a desire or goal begins as a seed thought accepted in the mind. A child needs to be nurtured, appreciated and protected. Just think how a mother believes her child is the prettiest baby. She won't allow anyone to breathe on her baby and harm the new life with germs. Similarly, you have to breathe life into your dreams, believe they are the best, act upon them, and protect them from negative thoughts and people who would tell you that your goals are stupid or ridiculous. Don't let them breathe on your "baby."

Just like children need discipline and guidance, you need to follow through on your goals. Don't be distracted to go play.

Just like children need emotional support, you will need positive support and encouragement so you won't give up on your goals.

Children are protected from bad associations, other children, or environments that can negatively influence them. Watch who you associate with also. "Birds of a feather, flock together." If you spend too much time with people who are negative, with no ambition, or vision, you will be influenced by their life-style. Your goals will suffer.

You have to be flexible with children. My two sons have two different kinds of personalities. Each one requires a different approach & style of parenting. What works for one does not always work for the other. I've learned to be flexible instead of rigid. Your goals require flexibility. Each goal will have its own personality and requirements for proper fulfillment. Some goals may require more time than others.

My children have taught me many things. They have helped me to grow in many ways. In aspiring for my goals, my strengths and weaknesses have also been revealed. My goals have taught me about discipline, emotions, money, faith, determination and lessons of victory and failure. Goals and children can make you feel proud or crazy. They both need a lot of attention.

COSMIC COMPANIONSHIP

Martin Luther King Jr. lived his spiritual walk in the midst of outer turmoil and attacks. He stated that because he was aware of a "cosmic companionship" in the form of God, he could still have inner calm. Martin Luther King Jr. was convinced of a living God that responded to the deepest yearnings of the human heart that answers prayers.

Martin Luther King, Jr.s' legacy reminds us that in spite of personal indignities, disappointments or struggle, to be aware of the "benign power..." a cosmic companionship... that never leaves us. Martin Luther King Jr. wrote "in the midst of lonely days and dreary nights, I have heard an inner voice saying, "Lo, I will be with you."

When you feel far from God, guess who has moved? I believe that because of our human experiences of fear, pain, ignorance or ego, we move in consciousness away from guidance, provision, comfort and love of God. When we become ONE with the power and companionship of God, we can bear the unbearable, think the unthinkable, see the invisible, conquer the immovable, reach the untouchable, and believe the impossible because of our faith.

Martin, Malcolm, Marcus and Mandela are among the many who succeeded in becoming and overcoming agonizing moments. We call them a success because of their unwaivering faith and life of action.

When you become aware of the cosmic companionship all around you, you will reach new heights of success in your personal, spiritual and professional life.

Men and women today are moving mountains and transforming their fears into years of dedicated purpose and passion. Convictions, goals, integrity, faith, good health, loving relationships and vision are required to climb to those mountains.

Just remember... between your vision and victory may be valleys. Don't be discouraged. Remember those who have gone before you taking on the yoke of God. This benign, infinite, all-knowing and wise power is your companion. Just stay!

SUCCESSFUL RELATIONSHIPS

After meeting someone new, and finding out you have the same astrological sign, or went to the same school, or read the same book, or that they look so good, or made you feel so good, have you said, "That's the ONE?" This is called "<u>falling</u> in love" and the relationship itself is based on limited information and interaction. When someone is emotionally, sexually or financially dependent on the other, it makes for a weak, toxic and short-lived relationship. Someone "falls" and is hurt because the relationship didn't have the benefit of time, patience, predetermined values and/or open communication. In some relationships, people "lean" while others may "lift."

"Rising (growing) in love" happens when two people are not just gazing into each others eyes, but are looking in the same direction. They share similar goals, interests and the characteristics listed below. Time, love and commitment will allow the whole person's personality to be revealed.

A desperate person makes desperate choices. The person who has developed self-esteem, self-acceptance and self-reliance is more likely to appropriately select instead of being selected. There are no guarantees that it will always work out. The chances are higher for a strong and long relationship if you seek compatibility in the listed qualities as opposed to settle for attraction in just one or two areas. An equally yoked relationship is created when there is attraction and compatibility in the following areas:

PHYSICAL - grooming, physical features, body/health care

RECREATIONAL - sport, leisure activities, social activities, outdoor/indoor activities, travel, movies

SEXUAL - values, intimacy style, expectations, fantasies, desires, romance, ability to show affection and sensitivity

EDUCATIONAL - What level of education is important to you in your mate? Do you share common interests in reading, school, seminars, or degrees?

INTELLECTUAL - Do you share common interest in current events, politics, culture, and the arts?

EMOTIONAL - control of negative emotions, healing from past unresolved issues, ability to share feelings, maturity

SPIRITUAL - similar views on religion and spirituality, practices, rituals, meditation, tithing, faith & prayer

FINANCIAL - spending habits, saving habits, earning abilities and earning potential. Is there secrecy, lying or conflict?

FAMILY - values, family history, culture, life-style, gender role expectations, socioeconomic status

10 THINGS TO REMEMBER ABOUT RELATIONSHIPS

1. No one relationship is completely fulfilling. Don't settle for half a person and try to make them whole. Don't go to the **ALTAR** hoping to **ALTER** your mate.

2. Learn how to communicate your feelings and goals. Help your mate to feel safe in communicating to you also.

3. Keep your 20's to yourself. Get to know yourself. Your likes and dislikes will change. You're still growing and searching for your identity. You're growing from a dependent relationship with parents into an independent life-style. Learn self-reliance and a healthy self-esteem before you enter into an interdependent relationship. Take time to accumulate wealth, get your education, pay your own bills, travel, and take care of your own personal and domestic needs. Learn how to be secure in your own solitude. The more patience and time you give to this developmental stage, the less likely you are to become a needy person emotionally, sexually or financially.

4. Write down the goals and values you seek. What are you ready to expect, accept and reject in a relationship?

5. Let friendship be a building block for your relationship.

6. Be real... so that love can heal and reveal.

7. Heal your emotional "stuff" from past, painful, unresolved amily issues and past relationships.

8. Don't have unrealistic expectations that one person can solve your problems, heal your pain or fulfill all your needs. Be strong and secure within yourself, so that you do not become a needy or naive person.

9. Don't kiss a fool, and don't let a kiss fool you. Sex is not love. Love is not sex. Learn to discern between like, love and lust.

10. Healthy and loving relationships require work, quality time, commitment, love and communication. You must adapt to "we," not just "me." Less ego and more of God can guide you in the ways of true unconditional love.

BEFORE YOU GET MARRIED...

An African proverb states, "Before you get married keep both eyes open and after you marry, close one eye."

Before you get involved and make a commitment to someone, don't let lust, desperation, immaturity, ignorance, pressure from others or a low self-esteem make you blind to warning signs. Keep your eyes open and don't fool yourself that you can change someone or that what you see as faults aren't really that important. Once you decide to commit to someone, over time their flaws, vulnerabilities, pet peeves and differences will become more obvious. If you love your mate and want the relationship to grow and evolve, you've got to learn how to close one eye and not let every little thing bother you. You and your mate have many different expectations, emotional needs, values, dreams weaknesses and strengths. You are two unique individual children of God who have decided to share a life together. Neither one of you are perfect, but are you perfect for each other? Do you bring out the best in each other? Do you compliment and compromise with each other or do you compete, compare and control? What do you bring to the relationship? Do you bring past relationships, past hurt, past mistrust, past pain? You can't take someone to the altar to alter them. You can't make someone love you or make someone stay. If you develop self-esteem, spiritual discernment and "a life" you won't find yourself making someone else responsible for your happiness or your pain. Manipulation, control, jealousy, neediness and selfishness are not the ingredients of a thriving, healthy, loving and lasting relationship. Seeking status, sex and security are the wrong reasons to be in a relationship.

What keeps a relationship strong?
•communication
•intimacy
•a sense of humor
•sharing household tasks
•some getaway time without business or children
•daily exchanges (a meal, shared activity, a hug, a call, a touch, a note)

•sharing common goals and interests
•giving each other space to grow without feeling insecure
•giving each other a sense of belonging and assurances of commitment
•asking God to be the center of your relationship

If these qualities are missing, the relationship will erode as resentment, withdrawal, abuse, neglect, dishonesty, and pain .

SEEK PROGRESS, NOT PERFECTION

Keeping a relationship strong and stress-less requires a lot of communication, trust, love-in-action, time, patience and prayer. The pressures of everyday living can kill the joy, hope, love and romance. If one of you becomes angry or stressed, the other becomes the closest target of their mate's frustration. Some people act out their frustration by withholding love and affection. Or they become abusive, domineering, critical, withdrawn, uncooperative, revengeful, crazy, lazy, indifferent, argumentative, depressed, unfaithful, dishonest or unforgiving. Choose your battles wisely. Some things are not worth fighting about. Ask yourself, "Do I want to be right or do I want peace?" Your loved one will stop coming home if it's a hassle instead of a castle. So work on keeping your heart open and spending quality time together to keep your relationship sweet and strong.

Relationships can be healed and renewed with some extra effort, prayer, improved communication, counseling, re-commitment to the union and some growing up! But there are some cases when a partner is holding on tooooo long. It's over, but they live on hope and illusion. When the signs of abuse, neglect, withdrawal, incompatibility or betrayal are there, it's time to pray for courage and self-esteem, and to take appropriate action. Is it time to interact, confront, "carefront", forgive, pray, grow or go? Denial, fear and obsessive "blind love" are very common and self-defeating. When you are willing to see the problem, then you're able to either heal or let go of the problem.

In order to have peace of mind and a fulfilling relationship, develop emotional boundaries that create and nurture respect, mutuality, care, peace, joy, communication and commitment. Don't assume that your mate knows what you want... speak up! Don't assume that the person you fell in love with will always remain the same. Times change. People change. You will change. The qualities and flaws, the virtues and vices that exist in both of you will be revealed over time. Neither one of you are perfect, but maybe you are perfect for each other. Learn to look for the true character of a person not just their looks, car, income, status or sex appeal. Value performance, not promises. Seek peace and progress, not perfection.

7 PEARLS FOR DAILY POSITIVE PRAYER...

WORRY... God is within me, around me, and protecting me, so I will let go of the fear that shuts out His guiding Light and makes me stumble into ditches of error and despair. Worry only changes one thing... ME. I am easily and divinely guided to solve my challenges.

FINANCES... My good comes from expected and unexpected channels. I have more money coming in than going out. I am a responsible and wise money manager. I work, save, invest and tithe to keep money circulating to me and others. All my financial needs are met and I pay all my debts because I know that God is MY source.

LOVE... I am a loving and forgiving person. Therefore, I attract loving and supportive relationships. I experience love wherever I go. The people I am seeking are also seeking me. I am never alone.

CAREER... My skills, talents and actions create the right employment and income for me. My work is challenging and fulfilling. I am created to be successful. My service creates value and a great income to meet my financial needs. I work with and for wonderful people who appreciate my work.

HEALTH... I see my body healthy, active and beautiful. Wellness is my priority because I know it is a precious temple where the Spirit of God resides. Therefore, I treat it with respect, healthy foods, water, exercise and loving thoughts. I take good care of my body. It is the only one I have.

ATTITUDE... I choose my thoughts with care. I am in the process of positive change. I know that I will get in life whatever I love, fear or expect. I keep my thoughts focused on good. I am grateful for my blessings. My life is getting better and better every day. I am excited about being in control of my life. Today is a great day...I will make it so.

LOVED ONES... Those I love are surrounded by God's presence, protection and supply. I release any anxiety about their well-being. I will not blame, criticize or condemn. I say to them, "Your way may not be my way, but I trust the Spirit of God in you to show you the way to your highest good."

DIAMONDS IN THE ROUGH

Every diamond has a flaw. Even though diamonds are brilliant, reflect light and are one of earth's most precious stones, they have imperfections. The untrained eye may not see the flaws, but a master gemologist can detect them. The cut, color, clarity and carat weight determine the quality of the diamond.

Just like diamonds, we have flaws, imperfections and deficiencies to strengthen. As a diamond in the rough, life's experiences of pain, grief, setbacks and disappointments cut and shape our character. Each cut (experience) has the potential to make us stronger. As we develop clarity and inner strength, our character builds. Our Master knows that we have flaws. We are not asked to be perfect, just grow and be our best.

I believe the book of Galatians chapter 5, verse 22, is one of our character building guides to polish up our "diamond in the rough" immaturity. We are reminded in Galatians that the fruits of the Spirit are:

love	joy	gentleness
peace	patience	self-control
kindness	goodness	faithfulness

You can enjoy success in emotional mastery by studying and embracing these qualities. When you are new on a sports team, in a new relationship, an adolescent making your passage into adulthood, a new employee on the job, a new student on campus, in a higher position on the job or new public servant, you are a "diamond in the rough." Don't stress yourself out striving for perfection. Mistakes are natural when you are growing. Turn the negative into positive, and learn from each mistake. You will learn to value each one as your character builds.

The Master doesn't focus on your flaws, so you shouldn't focus on your flaws and shortcomings either. Instead focus on your value, beauty, strength and ability to reflect the Light. The diamond becomes more and more radiant as it undergoes friction and pressure. When life brings you pressure and friction, remember the fruits of the Spirit. For heaven's way is to sharpen without cutting. You can endure. It's time to rise and shine!

GET EVEN WITH THOSE
WHO HAVE HELPED YOU

The emotional trap of wanting to get even with those who have hurt you serves no purpose. When people would ask me what I would do if I ever became successful, I answer, "Get even with those who have **helped** me." Sure there have been people who disappointed me, criticized me, condemned me, questioned me and tried to misuse me. **HOWEVER,** there have also been wonderful people in my life, sometimes whom I least expected, that have been supportive and caring while I built my career. Friends, family, students in my Enlightened Circle Classes and professionals have provided me with encouragement, prayers, contacts, referrals, clothes, money, transportation, flowers, cards, volunteer work, stamps and professional services. I choose to **remember, repay** and **return** those positive blessings because I can't afford to waste my energy and anger on the negative.

Revenge, resentment and anger are toxic emotions. Anger is just one letter short of (d)anger. If others have tried to block your success or peace of mind, realize you don't have to accept their messages or judgement of you. A way to successfully cope with this is to "insulate" yourself. The scripture reminds us to put on our "armor of light." When you surround yourself with positive associations and have a healthy self-esteem, a person's negative words and intentions can't penetrate your armor. They won't be able to get into your head or soul and rob you of serenity, determination and love.

In the second part of this book are suggested affirmations for you to learn. Repeating these positive declarations can strengthen you mentally and spiritually.

There are many good people in the world. There are many good people in **your** world who are ready to help you when they see you helping yourself. Some people will come into your life for a reason. They may be there for a certain purpose, and the time may be short-lived. Others may come into your life for a season. They also are there for a certain purpose, but the time is longer and sweeter. Giving back to those "angels" in your life who have assisted you or nurtured you is one of the keys to success called **reciprocity**.

WORDS CAN HEAL

Using these words and phrases can <u>increase</u> your chances for success and happiness:

I am special
I am unique
I feel good about myself
I work on improving myself
I keep my commitments
I am beautiful
I radiate confidence
I have a purpose
I am significant and needed
I am healthy
I am loved
I am responsible
I am strong
My challenges are my teachers
I'm willing to learn
I trust my inner voice
I'm always in the right place at the right time
I can solve my challenges
I believe in my skills and talents
I can get the job done
I expect great things to happen
I am qualified
I am worthy
I accept myself the way I am

Positive self-talk and conversations are attractive qualities. Yes... you can learn to be self-assured and confident <u>instead of</u> egotistical, self-centered and cocky. Positive words affect your health, reduce stress and create peace of mind. You can attract or repel healthy relationships and opportunities, according to your words. Life is a mirror. You attract into your life what you radiate, think, say, give and love.

Your positive inlook will shape your outlook in life. If you are optimistic and understand the power of your spoken word, your chances for success and solutions are more likely than for the person who speaks negativity.

WORDS CAN HARM AND HURT

Using these words and phrases will <u>decrease</u> your personal power for success:

There are no men
All men are dogs
There are no good jobs
There are no good women around
It's just no use
There's just no way
Nobody likes me
I'm too shy
I can't remember anything
He/she makes me sick, they are a pain in the neck
I hate my job
I hate my life
I can't trust anybody anymore
I never know what to do
I never get a break
If I start a business, I'll probably fail
I don't have any talent
Someone always hurts me
It doesn't matter what I say
It doesn't matter what I think
I knew it wouldn't work
I'm too ugly, fat, and stupid
It's too late to change
I don't deserve to be loved
Drugs and alcohol can't hurt me
Nobody will miss me if I die
I can't take care of myself

This kind of negative self-talk and attitude lowers your self-esteem. It creates dis-ease in your body and repels others who want to be close to you or help you.

When you change your <u>inlook</u>, it changes your <u>outlook</u> on life. Change your inner self-talk. Change your conversations with others. Self-acceptance and positive thinking are attractive qualities. Words and thoughts are vibrations registered in every cell of your body. If you keep saying you're sick and broke, you feel the stress. Headaches, ulcers, high blood pressure, violence, and depression, are the result. Think twice before you speak. And remember, "What you talk about... you will bring about."

THE ESSENCE OF GEMSTONES

Gemstones are manifestations of light, color, texture, vibrancy, transparency and clarity. The stones are crystallized through heat and pressure. Egyptian priests left manuscripts showing the system of color science. The solar energy of the sun is stored in the hue-man body, flowers, and precious gems reflecting the seven colors of the rainbow. Gems are gifts from Mother Earth for adornment, rituals, and balancing the seven energy points in our bodies of light, vibration, and matter.

RED-GARNET- energy point is the base of the spine, connection to Mother Earth (red earth)
Attributes- brings circulation to normal, purifies, balances awareness and well being, reduces fears of insecurity, and draws out negativity

ORANGE-CARNELIAN- energy point is the spleen and reproductive organs
Attributes - physical power, courage and stimulates appetite and energy

YELLOW-CITRINE- energy point is the solar plexus (navel)
Attributes- provides a sense of stability, increases energy, stimulates the intellect, wisdom and intuition

GREEN-EMERALD- energy point is the heart
Attributes- strengthens memory, clear sight, harmony, sense of compassion and prosperity

BLUE-AQUAMARINE- energy point is the throat
Attributes- protection on or near water, purifies, cleanses, calms, soothes, stimulates inner quiet and peace, relates to the power of the spoken word

INDIGO-SAPPHIRE- energy point is the 3rd eye (mid forehead)
Attributes- cleanses negative mental status, aids in abstract concepts, opens mind to spiritual awareness and knowledge

VIOLET/PURPLE-AMETHYST- energy point is the top of head/crown
Attributes- creates pure thoughts, higher values and insight; radiates wealth, sacredness, confidence, royalty and beauty, represents a Oneness with the Creator

VOCABULARY FOR SUCCESS

If you want to experience more success and accomplish your goals... make these words a part of your daily routine and mental attitude:

FOCUS - a center of activity, attraction or attention

CONCENTRATE - to bring or direct toward a common center or objective, to place one's efforts, powers, attention on a problem

ACTION - a thing accomplished over a period of time, in stages, or with the possibility of repetition; initiative; an act of will; the most vigorous, productive, or exciting activity in a particular field, area or group; something done or affected

GOAL - the end toward which effort is directed; intention; a steady progressive realization toward a predetermined worthy idea

FAITH - allegiance to duty or a person; belief and trust; firm belief in something for which there is no proof; complete confidence; strong conviction

STRATEGY - the art of devising or employing plans toward a goal

PURPOSE - something set up to be attained; intention; resolution; determination; meaningful aim

DIRECTION - guidance of action or conduct; the line or course on which something is moving or is aimed to; a channel or direct course of thought or action

MOTIVATION - internal drive to accomplish desired results; a need or desire that causes a person to **act**

GEMOLOGY

My Father loved people and loved to talk about philosophy, the conditions and solutions of the black community. He also loved to talk about his love for his family. We share the same interests, so I guess it's true, the apple doesn't fall too far from the tree.

I didn't begin my speaking career until after his passing. After reading some of his books left in the store, I became fascinated with gemology. I have since shared with my audiences nationally as a keynote or workshop presenter, the following metaphors about diamonds and how it relates to the human experience.

Human	Diamond
hidden talents	buried treasure
pain, disappointment	cut, shaped
self-improvement	polished, buffed
life has challenges and pressures	diamonds undergo pressure
spirituality	reflects light
multi-talented	many facets of color
self-esteem/worth	valuable, precious
individual uniqueness	rare
no one is perfect	flaws, imperfections
focused intent	some are crystal clear
light, vibration, matter	light, vibration, matter

THE MAIN THING

Whenever I share with my audiences across the nation my life's theme, "The main thing... is to keep the Main thing... the **MAIN THING!**" I always receive a humorous response. On the surface it sounds cliche. But the reality of this affirmation is that this kind of attitude produces results.

So many times, one experiences frustration, fatigue and failure because their "plate is too full." One must learn to prioritize. Choose the project, goal or activity that is most important to you right now. Once you choose, make a commitment to that decision. The ability to let go of low priority goals, and the courage to commit to a decision, are the attributes of a winner.

This powerful attribute is what athletes experience on the football field, baseball field or basketball court. The players train themselves to tune out personal problems, household chores, the news, physical pain, poor weather or any distracting elements.

Life is likened to a game. Once you decide to stop being a spectator and become a participator... you have to develop a game plan, focus on your goal, listen to your coach, tune out the opposing spectators and be willing to handle resistance and tackles.

Keeping the main thing, the MAIN Thing, gives you purpose. However, your purpose won't last long without the passion. If you really love and enjoy not only the goal (destiny), but also the journey, you won't give up so easily when the game gets tough. I experienced immeasurable success once I developed this attitude of action, concentration and commitment. It is my sincere wish for you that you also accomplish your dreams and goals. Read this material often to keep yourself moving towards your greater good.

40 VALUABLE LESSONS THAT I'VE LEARNED

1. Relationships don't end, they change.
2. You CAN make a living doing what you love.
3. Never spend all you have.
4. In bad times, everyone can't help you and in good times, everyone isn't as happy for you. Learn how to discern and develop true friends.
5. Don't make promises to your children you can't keep.
6. God is always listening, be careful with your inner self-talk.
7. People and creditors have long memories.
8. The past has passed, let go of the pain, nostalgia, woulda, coulda, shoulda.
9. Practice everyday saying and/or doing something that is loving, helpful & purposeful.
10. Unrealistic expectations create frustrations.
11. I am too blessed to be stressed, don't sweat the small stuff.
12. Most people are not bad or mad, they are just sad and don't know how to get the love and attention they deserve.
13. Everything you say and think has power to create it's likeness. Fear and procrastination are major enemies of success.
14. God loves me.
15. Don't ignore or mistreat people, everyone is important.
16. Don't give up 5 minutes before your miracle.
17. Good health is so valuable, fragile, and a blessing. Drink a lot of water.
18. Don't take everything so serious, have a sense of humor.
19. People like to help or do business with people they already know,
20. but networking is critical. Meet and serve as many people as you can.
21. You didn't die from your mistakes, but you may have to repeat them if you didn't learn the lesson.
22. Read more, watch TV less.
23. Stay away from negative, critical, judgmental, gossipy people.
24. Spend as much time as possible around nature and beautiful environments.

25. Sometimes things you can't learn in a book or from a parent, teacher or pastor, you have to experience for yourself.

26. Acknowledge your shortcomings and work to improve them. Acknowledge your strengths, be humble without diminishing or denying them.

27. Stay focused to get a job done. Either do it, delegate it or dump it.

28. I didn't die from the painful times in my life, they made me stronger.

29. Don't let a fool kiss you. Don't let a kiss fool you. Kisses aren't promises.

30. Have a life, don't depend on others to make you happy and fulfilled.

31. God is too big to fit into one religion, God is everywhere and in everything.

32. Marriage and parenting are serious commitments, don't be in a hurry.

33. Find ways to show appreciation to those you love and care about, not just on holidays or birthdays.

34. Pay attention to details and keep good records.

35. Prayer changes things. Trust God's divine plan.

36. If you take it, return it. If you break it, fix it. If you know it, live it. If you want it, ask for it. If you use it, clean it. If you wear it, hang it up. If you made a mistake, take responsibility for it. If you have some, share it. If you own it, protect it. If you love someone, show it. If you believe it, you can achieve it.

37. Time is precious... live everyday to it's fullest... everyday is a special occasion.

38. Learn to enjoy your own solitude.

39. People come into your life for a reason or a season. They bring joy and lessons.

40. Always stay in the light in spite of any bad news or changes. This positive attitude will help you stay in peace rather than fall to pieces.

10 STEPS FOR SUCCESS

1. PEN and PAPER - Give your time and mind an assignment. Write down your goals. Be specific, realistic and have a target date. Write down your goals for income, lifestyle, work, health, home, relationships, etc. Think big and keep your goals visible and aligned with your values, desires, talents and lifestyle. Review and update your goals often.

2. PEOPLE - People can help or hinder your success. Surround yourself with positive, supportive, productive and like-minded people. Nurture your personal and professional relationships for balanced living. Make time for family and friends. Don't get so busy making a living...that you forget about living.

3. PASSION AND PURPOSE - What makes you feel alive and meaningful? The opposite of being bored and without direction is being "on point and on fire" about where you focus and invest your energy and resources. Enthusiasm, focused attention and a compelling desire to act on an idea is a powerful creative force that produces progress and fulfillment. Your passion and purpose will take you out of a "comfort zone" into a "creative zone". You can create results, if you add some action to your passion.

4. PRACTICE WISE TIME AND MONEY MANAGEMENT Seek ways to be efficient, productive and aware of how, when, who, why and where you give your time... and how you $ave, $pend and produce money. Be a good steward with the resources of time, credit and money.

5. PERSEVERANCE and PATIENCE - Success is a process. Seeking perfectionism or instant gratification is not practical or realistic. Don't procrastinate or become paralyzed by fear, setbacks and discouragement. Focus on what you're going to....not what you're going through. Remember the payoff when you finish and reach your goal. Cope with the changes in life with a positive and flexible attitude. Keep your attention on your intentions! The main thing...is to keep the Main Thing.... THE MAIN THING!

6. ENCOURAGE AND SERVE OTHERS - Mentor and serve others with compassion, love and excellence. Experience the joy and power of giving. The best and blessed must be willing to help the rest.

7. PRAYER - Prayer changes things. Faith is the ability to not panic. Quiet time and prayer restores your sanity, serenity and guides you to solutions. Pray for guidance, wisdom and strength. Free your mind of fear, self-condemnation, temptations, stress and worry. Practice an attitude of gratitude. Get spiritually renewed. Read "You Are Too Blessed" by Jewel Diamond Taylor.

8. BUILD CHARACTER - Develop inner qualities of honesty, fairness, integrity, self-esteem, reliability, self-discipline and respect for others. Acknowledge and work on your shortcomings and vices. Acknowledge and demonstrate your strengths and virtues.

9. ADD QUALITY - Be above average. Do more than expected. Give more than expected. Seek ways to add quality to your relationships, work performance, education, wardrobe, grooming and health care. Don't be lazy or take shortcuts to success. Put in the extra effort.

10. HEALTH IS WEALTH - Develop healthy habits of drinking water, exercise, healthy foods, sufficient rest and pleasant thoughts. Make time for your creativity and enjoy nature. Seek ways to improve your emotional well-being to overcome depression, low self-esteem, grief and stress. Be proactive vs. reactive in your health care check-ups, daily supplements and lifestyle choices (food, sex, addictions, work, commuting, clutter and stress).

FIND YOUR ZONE

Are you "on fire" with your life? Do you look forward to each day? Do you have enthusiasm on your job, at school or home? What do you do that puts you in a "zone?" I'm talking about a natural high!!! When I perform my work of speaking, writing, talking with people or listening to great music... I'm in a "zone." I don't feel any pain. I don't care what time it is. I don't feel hungry. I feel invincible. I feel unspeakable joy.

It took many years of soul searching, crazy/boring jobs, working on my dream part time while raising two sons to finally discover my purpose. Living my purpose keeps me sane and out of trouble. I have a life. This "zone" experience is different for everybody. For some people it is working on their music, art, poetry, writing, cooking, teaching, dancing, braiding hair, surfing the Internet, reading, traveling or playing basketball.

The point I'm trying to make is... find your "zone." Get that natural high that takes your mind off of your problems. When you're there, it even helps your immune system and your blood pressure. Being in that "zone" makes you a happier and healthier person. When you are creating and occupied with a purpose and activity that keeps you busy and focused, you can experience a satisfaction and an unspeakable joy that so many people are missing in their lives.

WHO'S SHAPING YOUR THOUGHTS?

The company you keep is important. Think about it. If you leave your coat in a room where people are smoking, pretty soon it will smell of smoke. You can have on the best cologne or perfume, but enough exposure to any different strong scent can over power the beautiful one you have one.

Such is the case with your mind. Your "garment of thoughts" absorbs the thoughts of those with whom you associate.

Whose thoughts are you wearing? If your thoughts had a scent, what would it be? Is it stinking thinking or beautiful thoughts of peace, harmony, success, faith and love?

Who shapes your thoughts?
Answer: Parents, TV, friends, spouses, lovers, co-workers, media, society, school, church, job, social organizations, etc.

When you find yourself around gossipy-critical-negative-complaining-little faith-much drama-reactive people, either you fit in and speak their language or you gravitate towards another kind of people and conversation that is positive, productive, progressive, solution-oriented, loving, creative, hopeful, caring and proactive.

As you grow older and wiser, you'll soon realize there are some people and some places you can't afford to hang around for the sake of your emotional, spiritual, and mental health. This is a success law for living.

IS YOUR LIFE OUT OF BALANCE?

There is nothing wrong with the pursuit of profit, prestige and power. It does become a problem when the pursuit is out of balance with the wrong motives. You can find yourself losing your mind and so much more when your life is out of balance.

A pursuit of your life's purpose, peace and a passion for God, family and humankind is the alternative. This kind of life becomes an irresistible positive force and magnet drawing to it all things.

Socrates taught that the biggest battle we fight is on the battle-ground divided between "I want" and "I should." This is the inner warfare.

In order to avoid dangerous pursuits of self-righteousness and create a truly rich life, one must do the inner soul work. I strive everyday for this balance as I am sure you do also. I put on my armor of Light and go into inner warfare to overcome what the body and mind seeks (comfort, approval, the path of less resistance, pro-crastination, ego, gratification from sugar, sex, sleep, shopping, pity-party, etc.)

We can begin when we give ourselves quiet time to turn off the voices of home, the media, family, society, work and friends. Learning to hEAR with the "spiritual ear" takes practice. It helps us to reacquaint ourselves with our rhythms, personal sessions of trials, triumph and tests, our wounds, hopes, memories and aspirations.

Create a space and a place in your home, and during the day while at work or school, separate yourself from the busy-ness and business of the day. Be still, be quiet, exhale, pray, refocus, review your priorities, reach out to someone special in your life and renew yourSelf.

ENJOY LIFE NOW

When feelings of inadequacy like (I'm too fat, I'm too stupid, Nobody likes me, I can't win, It's too late, I'm too ugly, What if I fail?) are in your mind and in your conversations, you are limiting yourself and putting yourself down. Psyche yourself UP like Muhammed Ali did by saying and believing, "I am the greatest." You've got to believe in yourself.

Sure, you're not perfect... but no one is. It's alright to observe your shortcomings. Improve them, just don't dwell on them. The very thing you keep focusing on, probably no one is paying attention to it. You may have gained a few pounds; or started to go a little bald; or you're shy; or maybe you're recently divorced; or your education isn't completed yet; or maybe you had some past misfortune; or you only have a couple of dollars in your wallet... no one knows it but you. Don't walk around with a big sign advertising and pointing out your flaws and issues for everyone to see. Everybody around you is dealing with some type of issue in their life. They're too busy trying to fix their life to be worried about your issues too. Get over it and get busy living and enjoying life. Do you have excuses or enthusiasm? Do you know that if you think you can't... you can't and if you think you can, you can?

ARE YOU IGNORING GOD'S HELP?

After a tremendous down pour of rain, people were instructed by radio broadcast to vacate their homes. One woman refused and said the Lord would take care of her. A man came by in a car and encouraged her to get out and save herself from the impending flood. The woman's response was that she was already "saved" and her faith would not allow her to give up so easily. After a while another man came by in a boat, again encouraging her to get in because the water was quickly rising. She refused saying that she was a praying woman believing God would protect her and her home. More time passed and more rain fell. A helicopter flew above her home and dropped her a line. The pilot shouted, "Come on lady, you're crazy, you're gonna drown in this flood, get in!" She stood on the roof shouting, "God will save me. I'm not leaving my home." It continued to rain and unfortunately she drowned. When she arrived in heaven, she couldn't wait to ask God why He allowed her to die. "Why did you forsake me Lord when I was depending on you, praising your name and standing on my faith on my roof?" God replied, "I sent you a car. I sent you a boat. I sent you a helicopter. I didn't forsake you, I am always with you. I did not ignore you... you ignored ME! I work in many mysterious ways to inspire, provide, guide and rescue you from danger."

Isn't that true? The very thing you're praying for, seeking and asking for comes disguised as... work, a person, an opportunity, a pain, an idea, a dream, a relationship, a child, a question, a song, a book, a movie, a sign on the road, a sermon/lecture, a tip, a conversation, an invitation, a dream, an e-mail, etc.

When you get what you're asking for, do you ignore it or say "I can't believe it!" Perhaps you say, "It's too good to be true" or "I thought it was going to be easier or different or taller or faster". Or are you spiritually blind to the ways of the Creator and need a big NEON FLASHING SIGN saying, "Here I AM?"

JEWEL'S POETRY GEMS

THE REAL ME

I'm coming from behind my mask
learning to love myself real fast.
So many times I've given my power away
to fear and what others would think or say.

I'm learning it's OK to receive and to ask.
I'm getting my self-esteem and power back
I learn from my pain and discover who I really am.
I'm getting free from my "mental jam."

No longer scared, unfulfilled or a fake.
My self-worth and confidence, no one can take.
It <u>does</u> matter what I think, do and say.
I now know that I'm really OK.

I'm removing this mask of fear.
I deserve success, happiness and love so dear.
It's time to really be ME.
A strong and positive woman you'll see.

How great it is to be alive in this universe.
This life of mine I no longer curse.
No time for self-doubt or feeling blue.
I've got dreams and goals to pursue.

Here I am victorious, beautiful and free.
This Queen will rise and shine because
courage, strength and wisdom abide in me.

I'm coming from behind my mask
living in truth and the Light at last!

LIFE IS...

Life is a journey...   walk it
Life is a gift...   open it
Life is a flower...   smell it
Life is a ball...   catch it
Life is a song...   sing it
Life is a mystery...   discover it
Life is painful...   endure it
Life is beautiful...   see it
Life is wonder-full..   enjoy it
Life is precious...   don't waste it
Life is unlimited...   go for it!
Life is love...   give it
Life is light...   shine in it
Life is God in you..   rejoice in it!

COUNT YOUR BLESSINGS

Count your blessings, not your bruises.
Count your friends, not your foes.
Count your opportunities, not your obstacles.
Count your miracles, not your mistakes.
Count your dreams, not your disasters.
Count the hours of light, not the hours of the night.
Count the diamonds in Mother Earth, not the rocks in the dirt.

Count all those who said, "I love you,"
Not the ones in a bad mood.

Count all the times God brought you through,
Not the things He didn't do.

BLACKITUDES

RESURRECT your rich African history.

REMEMBER your ancestors struggle, sacrifice and success.

RECLAIM our power as a people by getting involved.

RENEW your self-esteem, self-respect and self-worth.

REBUILD your communities, keep them clean and buy property.

REFUSE to be a part of the problem in the community.

REDUCE black-on-black crime and be a part of the solution.

READ to educate yourself and others because knowledge is power.

RECYCLE & REINVEST dollars to increase economic strength.

REACH back to help others less fortunate.

RADIATE your light to promote love, unity and peace.

RESCUE our youth with love, mentoring and positive examples.

RESPECT your elders and learn from their experience.

REJOICE in your greatness and contributions to the world.

RAISE your consciousness to know truth and rise above negativity.

REALIZE the melanin and genius of Kings, Queens, leaders and survivors who are in your genes to help you create and succeed!

LOYAL TO MY ROYAL PAST

I must remember to be loyal to my royal past.
I must not forget we were first... and not last.
Stories of my ancestors are carved on the pyramid walls.
They were creative, innovative and stood so tall.
My hand rocked the cradle when civilization began.
Diamonds and riches are buried in the womb of my dark land.
My full breasts have fed all mankind.
I carry the black seed for generations in time.
I dance to the drum. I sing and hum the songs I wrote like,
"Oh Mary Don't You Weep..." "Old Ship of Zion" and
"Sometimes I Feel Like a Motherless Child."

My bones from slave trade lay in a wet grave
at the bottom of the sea.
And I have swung as strange fruit from a tree.
I have made art, inventions, maps, calendars and sweet love.
I have toiled the land and dried up like a raisin
from the hot sun above.
My children and I have bathed in the Nile.
I have crossed the Sahara for many a mile.

With my brother and sister, I have been stoned, bombed
and walked when I'd rather ride the bus.
I have prayed and marched for justice.

My Father is the Sky. My Mother is the Earth.
My son is the sun. My daughter is the moon.
My aunts are Sojourner, Harriet, Nefertiti, Mary and Isis.
My uncles are Frederick, Marcus, Malcom, Martin, Horus,
Rasul and Solomon.

I am a healer. I am a teacher. I am a leader. I am a fabric weaver
of kente. I am a dancer. I am a braider of woolen hair. I am a
drummer. I am a survivor.
My history is written on my grandmother's quilt
and I am still here... like the pyramids I built.

SONG FOR THE BLACK MAN

Loving message for the black man
fashioned and formed by Spirits' hand,
seed carrier from the Motherland,
you built the pyramids that still stand.

You are not made of snakes, snails and puppy dog tails.
You are designed to build, lead, succeed and not fail.
You are made of the Creator's strength, wisdom and love.
You are made from the clouds, water, earth and sun above.

You have feelings deep inside to express.
It's time to release, open up and confess.
When you learn to support and confide in your brother.
You'll discover a friend in him like no other.

Reach out to each other in times of pain and confusion
to help each other to cast out all illusion.
Don't let fear and ego make your heart a stone.
It's not your macho pride or muscles that always need to be shown.

You are not made of snakes, snails and puppy dog tails.
Don't stand alone on the corner or locked away in the jails.
Knowledge, love, unity and truth will set you free.
Remember, you alone hold the key.

Come out, come out and celebrate life
as a father, brother, son, friend or husband to your wife.
Remember these qualities to your queen you should give
sense of humor, responsible, spiritual and sensitive.

Talking and listening builds a strong relationship.
Make sure the foundation is based on friendship.
Groom and love her by being a God-directed man
and by your side... she will always stand.

SEE SISTER

See Sister reflection of First Mother carrying the black seed.
She loves her family and people, takes care of their needs.
Hear sister, talking to God saying, "Lord, I'll do all I can,
      but please lend your helping hand."

See sister adorning her rich hue with jewels and fabric divine.
It drapes her curves, emotional scars and sensuous lines.
See sister, she can wear something old and make it look new.
      She's always moving and got something to do.

Honor sister, sacrificing, struggling and working for truth.
She's always willing and saying... "What can I do?"
Study sister providing milk from her mountains,
wisdom from her mind and life from her hips.
      She never seems to find time to just sit.

Proud, full in body, pyramid nose, hair of wool, tigress of strength,
and soul of the moon.
      She's the **african violet** in full bloom.

See sister, nubian, chocolate and sweet.
But don't make her mad or step on her feet.
Even though tired.... she still works and walks with the legacy.

See sister...... she's just like you.
She wants peace... a home... and a love so true.
Listen to sister, she may <u>not</u> tell you she's in pain.
Next time... take time, listen, hug and help her to feel sane.

Even though she may seem distant, different, defensive or bold.
You don't know what her life's story would be... if it were told.
We've all done different things to survive, to be loved & accepted.
It's painful to be continually judged, denied and rejected.
Since life offers joy and pain from the beginning to the end,
let's show compassion and learn how to be true sisterfriends.

Woman wise and sister strong, Caribbean, African and American
See sister, **respect** sister, **love** sister... understand?

DAUGHTERS OF THE FIRST WORLD

Black women your history is real.
You are made of velvet and steel.
You were the first to be kissed by the sun.
With your **mind**, all obstacles you can overcome.
Your **body** is adored, with its fullness and rich hue.
Your **spirit** guides you in your dreams to pursue.
You're a radiant diamond from the Motherland.
In spite of life's pressures... you continue to stand.

Your creativity and faith sustain you to survive.
Sojourner and Harriet inspire you to keep hope alive.
You are caregivers, teachers, leaders and homemakers.
You are artists, students, entrepreneurs and policy makers.
You are on the go... movers and shakers.

Remember, in unity we are more wise, rich and strong.
If we all "stay in the Light"... we can't go wrong.
Strength and wisdom... our ancestors continue to send.
So Queens... let's be loyal to the royal within.
Don't let anyone or anything take your smile or crown.
Let's encourage each one to be more positive and not frown.

Daughters of the first world painted on the pyramid walls,
be proud and never cease hearing your native drum call.
For there is much to do to heal our cultural wounds.
Gather your energy from God, the sun and the moon.
Our communities and family need nurturing so much.
It's our minds and hands that provide that healing touch.

YOU ARE PRECIOUS

You are a beautiful diamond refined from black coal.
You're precious and have more value than silver or gold.

You're like a diamond who has pressure and friction...
so don't give up... just stay with your mission.

Don't worry and count all your mistakes.
Every diamond has a flaw, whether real or fake.

Look for the positive in every negative situation.
Just like the oyster make pearls from its irritations.

There is a Higher Power within to help you sparkle and shine.
Begin now to go deeper, search and develop your mind.

The joy and happiness you'll find, you can't even measure
when you begin to seek and claim your treasure.

Your life will unfold with harmony... just seek and knock.
Be strong, clear and full of Light, like that precious rock.

Be your best, give your best and you'll gain all the rest.
Your life's journey can be so bright.
Be strong, overcome darkness and always "stay in the Light."

I'LL MEET YOU ON HIGHER GROUND

When you realize that you're more than just your body,
status and degree.
When you start believing in the Invisible Spirit
to overcome and achieve.
     I'll meet you on higher ground.

When you recognize your inherent value and self-worth.
When you realize that you are part of heaven and earth.
When you're ready to rise above man's ignorance and hate.
When you're ready to love unconditionally, it's never too late.
     I'll meet you on higher ground.

When you're letting Spirit direct your path and way.
When you're living with "blessed assurance"
every minute, hour and day.
When you begin to say, "I won't give up in spite of my setbacks."
When you claim God's abundance, and not the limit or lack.
     I'll meet you on higher ground.

When you see with your "enlightened eyes"
what others can't see.
And during uncertain times you affirm "Divine order" and
continue to believe.
     I'll meet you on higher ground.

When you won't let your sorrows and fears keep you down.
When you stop negative people and thoughts from coming around.
When you express love, unity, faith and peace.
     I'll meet you on higher ground.

When you recognize the Divine in You and Me
When you're ready... I'll be here... you'll see
so many waiting for you on higher ground.

WORK ON YOUR DREAMS TODAY

Today you have another chance to work on your dreams.
You can accomplish something today
before you lay your head down for rest
know that today you have given your best.
Though you may not know the meaning of it all,
don't hesitate, procrastinate or stall.
Be prepared, bold and ready
or this day you will be regretting
if your goals you are not setting.

You can write, make phone calls or read
meditate, study, network, plant seeds.
The seeds of your work will surely manifest
by giving, loving and working to bring your harvest.

Mining for diamonds takes persistence, work and time.
They are precious and valuable like your life and mine.
Therefore, be willing to work each day for your treasures.
The success and happiness you gain is beyond measure.

Sit under the learning tree today
to study and read what the mystics have to say.
Love their wisdom as they talk to you from book pages,
the innovators, leaders, history makers and sages.

Another day is here to work on your dreams and plans
to think about traveling to different lands,
Jamaica, Sedona, Hawaii's white sand or
to see the pyramids made by our forefather's hands.

Be calm, steady and poised
in spite of the world's madness and noise
for you are connected to something bigger than you or me
you're one with the One who gave you dreams to believe

Be thankful for your life, gifts and dreams
that flow abundantly from an endless stream.
Greet each day with thanksgiving and wonder
knowing it's God's love and grace you live under.

God is the giver of the dreams you dream today.
Have faith and trust that He'll make a way.

PROCRASTINATION IS A THIEF

Experience can be an expen$ive teacher in one's life.
Beware of a lesson that can bring stress and strife.

Procrastination is the lesson I'm talking about.
It's also a thief that can **cost** you an enormous amount.

It will try to be your friend and whisper "tomorrow."
Beware, listening to that **voice of delay** will cause you
great sorrow.

Don't put off taking care of business and paying that bill.
Pay attention to your body signals **before** you get seriously ill.

Procrastination can cause emotional, financial and physical pain.
By listening to this voice, you have nothing to gain.

Putting things off **doesn't** make them go away.
You'll have to face it, why not today?

Adding up each and every day are small nagging chores.
Do it now, before they multiply and become more.

Repair your car, start that project, return that call.
Do it now, or procrastination will lead to failure and fall.

Make a list, begin that class, change your ways, follow
through, protect your health, do it now, whatever your do.

There are new opportunities, and renewed energy waiting for you.
Get up, overcome fear and have a **"get-it-done"** attitude!

DON'T GIVE UP

GET UP... rise and shine each day. Let go of yesterday's sorrows and regrets. Greet this day with enthusiasm and an attitude of gratitude for how far you have come, and be thankful for a brand new start.

WAKE UP... don't be lazy or asleep to the opportunities you can seize. Shake off depression. This day holds great possibilities.

SHOW UP... with your presence and participation today at school, the job, your business or that special meeting because it is significant to your future. Be active, network and participate in activities that will empower you. No excuses today.

BRACE UP... prepare for the unexpected. Keep yourself spiritually grounded. Think ahead and do what is necessary to avoid pain, loss or confusion. Reality is subject to change without notice. So learn to be **proactive** instead of **reactive**.

THINK UP... a positive attitude is important. Think about productivity and progress. And think BIG. Have an expectancy of great things coming your way. You can do it!

BOUNCE UP... failure is not final. Cancel all pity parties. Learn how to recover quickly and begin again. Say to yourself, "This is temporary... this, too, shall pass." Take action to overcome feeling stuck, helpless or overwhelmed.

MEASURE UP... much is required of you today. Meet the challenge. Success requires time, quality, commitment, hard work and discipline.

KEEP UP... we live in an information age. Knowledge is power. Read, study, network, ask questions and master your particular field of interest.

DON'T GIVE UP

STAND UP... with conviction for what you believe. Be willing to defend what you believe in. Don't allow yourself to be a victim. Protect and defend yourself.

SPEAK UP... you are worthy. Learn the power of "asking". Overcome the fear of rejection. Learn how to communicate and articulate your desires, dreams and concerns. Learn how to sell and express your ideas.

REACH UP... to be taught by mentors, teachers, elders and those that will teach you how to avoid unnecessary mistakes. Ego and pride can be your worst enemy.

OPEN UP... to change and learn new ideas, meet new people and go new places. Don't get stuck in a rut... GROW!

POLISH UP... find ways to constantly improve your image, vocabulary, habits, working area, wardrobe and appearance. Think QUALITY and remember the true saying, "the first impression is a lasting impression."

STEP UP... to each task and follow through. Keep your commitments. Procrastination is a thief. Stay focused on the most important things that need to be accomplished today.

SAVE UP... "save money and money will save you" is an old Jamaican proverb. Financially successful people are able to respond to emergencies and opportunities. Develop financial wisdom which reduces stress and increases success.

LIVE UP... each day as a special occasion. Be good to yourself. Feel worthy of the "good life."

LOOK UP... remember the words of Psalms... "I will lift UP mine eyes unto the hills from whence cometh my help." During those dark uncertain times, endure, hold on and look to God within and above for your strength and guidance. Let your faith be strong, not weak.

POSITIVE THINKERS

*Positive Thinkers have **less stress**.*

Positive Thinkers are lovable people.

Positive Thinkers master their emotions.

*Positive Thinkers tend to **heal** faster.*

*Positive Thinkers have good **self-esteem**.*

Positive Thinkers usually do better with tests.

*Positive Thinkers feel **worthy** of asking for what they want.*

*Positive Thinkers attract positive and **supportive** friends.*

Positive Thinkers have "staying and praying" power.

Positive Thinkers enjoy the rose, in spite of the thorns.

Positive Thinkers see the glass half full, not half empty.

Positive Thinkers don't dwell on past mistakes.

*Positive Thinkers believe in **divine order**.*

Positive Thinkers don't take everything so personal.

Positive Thinkers do not judge by appearances.

*Positive Thinkers take **positive action** on their goals.*

*Positive Thinkers don't **sit** down when they have a **set** back.*

Positive Thinkers are willing to make changes and decisions.

*Positive Thinkers find **joy** by encouraging and helping others.*

Positive Thinkers know that complaining and worrying are a waste of time.

*Positive Thinkers know that when one door closes, another **will open**.*

*Positive Thinkers see **opportunities**, while others see obstacles.*

*Positive Thinkers focus on the **fullness** in their life, not the emptiness.*

Positive Thinkers work on themselves, and do not try to control others.

*Positive Thinkers count their **blessings, not their bruises**.*

Positive Thinkers count their friends, not their foes.

SUPERWOMAN TAKE OFF YOUR CAPE

Superwoman are you trying to do more and more and more?

Stress	Suicidal
Sister Strong	Student
Single parent	Self-esteem
Success driven	Struggling financial
Survivor	Single and Searching
Spiritual	Sane
Supporting and worrying	
about everybody else	

Take off your superwoman cape of red.
Don't feel guilty when it's time to rest a while in bed.

Don't try to do it all and wear yourself thin.

Pace yourself, delegate duties, let others pitch in.

Pat yourself on the back for how far you have come.
You're not lazy, unworthy, ugly or dumb.

Honor, nurture, love and protect yourself.
Act on your goals and take your dreams off the shelf.

You don't have to be a martyr, rescuer and save everyone.
Stress and fear will make you sick, depressed or numb.

More women are learning to let go of that "victim role."
Swallow your pride and ask for help to save your sanity and soul.

Don't isolate and feel you're all alone and weak.
It's time for your Power within and above to seek.

Take time off and renew, you deserve a temporary escape.
Superwoman... it's time to retire that cape!

WHO AM I?

Who am I? What makes me like no other?
Did I come from more than just the belly of my Mother?
Oh God, that I cannot see, tell me how did I come to be?

For I hear music like jazz, gospel, rock and roll
and I feel one with each note for it vibrates my very soul.
Well, that's me, I say in the music that I know.

I go to the park and lay in the green grass.
And I feel that I'm finally home at last.
Well, that's me in the beautiful healing grass.

I pass a stranger with a quick glance
I think... "is that me by chance?"
We stop and talk and share a while.
"That's me," I say, "in that stranger" beginning another mile.

I look up to the heavens and stars above.
The moon, jupiter, venus and mars.
Well, that's me up there, a shining star.

I go to the ocean and feel the ebb of the tide.
My mind, body and spirit just rejoice inside.
Well, that's me in those dancing waves that seem to glide.

I find diamonds and rubies in Mother Earth.
How precious they are.
Was that the beginning of my birth?
Well, that's me, a precious gem from the earth.

I look at my children so innocent and splendid (John & Jason)
They seem to ask the same questions that I did.
What a joy to watch them grow and become so much like me.
Well, that's me I say, in my child I see.

I stand still now and listen to my inner guide.
So thankful for all that You provide.
I now know... I'm more than just this body that I see.
I know you express through me. You express through every man,
bird, lake and tree. That's why I feel one with every-
thing I see. I know who I am now, I'm One with Thee.

ABC'S FOR SUCCESS

Action produces results
Believe in yourself and your dreams
Create the kind of life you desire and deserve
Discipline yourself to stay focused
Education expands your opportunities
Faith is the ability to NOT panic!
Grow beyond your fears and comfort zone
Health is your wealth, protect it!
Inspire and encourage others
Just get started, procrastination is a thief!
Keep the main thing, THE MAIN THING!
Live, laugh, love and learn everyday
Make time for self-renewal
Network and enlarge your circle
Open your heart and mind
Pray for guidance, wisdom and strength
Quality takes you to higher places
Remember, "don't give up, Stay in the Light"
Save and spend your money wi$ely
Time is precious, value your family and friends
Understand you can't change or control people
Verbalize, speak up, communicate your needs
Worry and complaining will steal your joy
Xccelerate your efforts, get self-motivated
You are too blessed to be stressed!
Zap the negative thinking and depression

DIAMOND AFFIRMATIONS

WHY DO AFFIRMATIONS HELP?

Anything you **do** repeatedly... anything you **hear** repeatedly... anything you **see** repeatedly... anything you **feel** repeatedly... anything you **think** repeatedly... anything you **say** repeatedly... has an affect on you internally and externally in your life's conditions.

If you keep lifting weights and exercising your physical muscles, your **physical** body gets stronger.

If you keep praying, studying the word, praising and living by faith, your **spiritual** body gets stronger.

If you keep reading, studying, thinking and solving problems, your **intellect** gets stronger.

One of the ways to become **mentally** strong in your beliefs is to repeatedly hear and say positive statements about the conditions you want to experience in your life. Your mind can do push ups and lift up the thoughts for higher expectations and performance. Constantly lifting your thoughts makes your mental will-power stronger against the weak thoughts of self-condemnation, procrastination and low self-esteem.

What you **believe** is determined by what your subconscious is exposed to by the environment, nutrition, conversations, past memories, books, news, media, peers, family, etc. Words, images and feelings make lasting impressions on your mind. If you don't like what you're experiencing in your life now, you can positively change the results by changing your **words, images** and **feelings** now.

On the following pages, I list some of the affirmations I find helpful to stay self-motivated. Read these daily.

AFFIRMATIONS FOR CHANGE AND LETTING GO

I trust that change brings good things.
I am a student of change.
I surrender to the flow of change.
I let go of resistance.
I am proactive vs. reactive in coping with my life.
I trust myself to adjust to change.
I am capable to make new decisions.
I am learning to adjust to new environments.
I am willing to surrender my comfort zone.
I am willing to explore new options.
I am willing to let go of the familiar.
I embrace new adventures.
I can overcome anxiety about change.
I can accept my feelings.
I will identify my resources and abilities.
I am willing to be responsible for my future.
I can start now taking steps to get what I want.

AFFIRMATIONS FOR MONEY AND PROSPERITY

Money is not the root of all evil. The <u>lack</u> of money or the <u>misuse</u> of money causes stress, havoc, pain, violence, low self-esteem and depression. Read these positive affirmations regularly to improve your financial health.

I am a money magnet.

I save money and money saves me.

I pay myself first.

I call forth my confidence.

I have positive cash flow and abundant har-money in my life everyday.

My work prospers me and others.

I associate with prosperous minded people.

I manage my time and money well.

I affirm increase for me and others.

I direct my energies toward my goal.

I develop my intuition and imagination to creatively solve all challenges.

I have more than enough money to thrive... not just survive.

I speak positive and think BIG. I take action on my ideas.

My conversation is positive about progress, possibilities and prosperity.

I believe in my talents, abilities and worth for financial wealth.

I have an attitude of gratitude.

I grow from my mistakes. I continue to grow in knowledge and experience.

I am worthy of money and success.

I am wealthy in mind, ideas, health, relationships, income and opportunities.

Nothing is too good to be true.

My mind is open to receive.

My cup runneth over. I am willing and glad to share and tithe.

People seek my services and products. I am successful in all my endeavors.

I am always in the right place at the right time. Everything is in divine order.

God provides me with inner peace, power, prosperity and provisions.

I have patience, enthusiasm, persistence and a plan for my greater good.

I am willing to make decisions and take action. I release all fear.

My faith and self-esteem are strong. I deny the negative messages and accept positive support and guidance.

I earn an excellent income that meets all my financial needs and lifestyle.

I am open to discover and create different ways of earning money.

Worry only changes one thing... ME. I release money stress. I am open to new ways to solve old problems.

I am willing to work and give quality in my service and/or products.

Money and opportunities are drawn to me from many different sources.

I now establish order in my financial affairs.

POSITIVE AFFIRMATIONS

INNER TALK for *YOUR DAILY WALK*/Positive Affirmations:

Today I will master my emotions.

When my faith is tested, I will not faint, fail or fall. I will look up and inward for my strength.

I do not take rejection and disappointment personal. When one door closes, I know another one will open.

I'm getting stronger every day in every way.

Today is a good day.

I will let go and let God.

I renounce all appetites, habits, values or thoughts which block the full intent and expression of God in my life now.

I am developing discipline to believe and achieve.

I welcome opportunities to serve and love others.

I am alert to opportunities.

I am organized.

I trust my ability to sell my products and/or service.

I am dependable.

My goals and purpose activate my internal success system.

Today I am focused on my priorities and possibilities.

I am a winner. I am a conqueror. I am an overcomer.

I am always guided to the best solutions.

My path is important.

I honor and use my special skills and abilities.

No person, no place, no thing can steal my joy today. I am the only thinker in my mind.

I am always in the right place at the right time.

Today I focus on the fullness in my life, not the emptiness.

Whatever I think about, I bring about.

I am comfortable making decisions and taking action.

I am successful. Others respect my work and my word.

Procrastination is a thief. I can... I will... I must be organized and follow through.

I feel good about my daily progress.

To develop good performance from others, I will develop praise, appreciation and encouragement skills.

Feeling bad is a waste of time.

I resolve not to share my problems with anyone unless they are part of the solution.

My income is constantly increasing. I see my good (money) coming from expected and unexpected channels.

My skills and talents create a great income for me to meet my financial needs and lifestyle.

I feed my body healthy foods and liquids. My body is my temple and transportation. Health is my priority. My health habits are improving each day.

My attitude of self-esteem is confident and loving.

I am friendly and trustworthy.

I train my mind to win.

Even though there may be appearances of lack, limitations and confusion...divine order is taking place in my life right now.

I will not give my power away with anger, jealousy, laziness, worry or bitterness.

I write down my goals and affirm them daily.

I surround myself with loving and positive people who are kind, helpful, on-the-grow and non-judgemental.

My growing is showing.

Spirit is everywhere and in everyone.

I am willing to allow happiness and hope to replace my grief and sadness. The darkness is lifting. I am walking in the light of a new day.

I am responsible for the quality of this day and my life.

Today I breathe in peace, balance, and love. I exhale tension, fear and dis-ease.

I'm expecting a breakthrough, <u>not</u> a breakdown.

I am a good time manager.

I use my time wisely.

I maintain balance with my personal and professional life. I make time for family and friends.

I have a get-it-done attitude. I am committed, consistent and complete each task with quality.

I'm ready for wonderful things to happen today. I give my full, alert attention to everything I do. God's love, power, presence and provision is active in my life!

I am centered in God's will for my life. I am secure in my individuality. I live in the fortress of God's inner presence. Today, I allow no one and no thing to steal my joy.

Today is a great day! I am alert to opportunities!

I am always guided to the best solutions.

I'm always in the right place, at the right time and prepared.

Worry doesn't change circumstances... it only changes me. Therefore, let go and let God.

I see my body healthy, active and beautiful. I treat it with respect, healthy foods, water, exercise and uplifting thoughts.

My skills and talents create the right job/business for me.

What I am seeking... is also seeking me. Therefore, I am mindful of what I think, believe, say and do.

Everything is in divine order. I release stress and accept success.

I train my mind for discipline, courage and action.

All obstacles are temporary. Stay in the Light!

I am willing to make decisions. I accept my responsibility for the quality of my emotional, financial, spiritual, physical and mental health. I am focused, capable and self-motivated!

I am surrounded with resources and opportunities. My good comes from unexpected people and places.

I am a money magnet. I am a wise money manager. I have more than enough money to maintain my life-style. I gladly give and receive money always.

I am unique. I radiate love, confidence, light and peace within and without my being.

Today I will endure and overcome all obstacles. I stay on higher ground in spite of challenges.

There are many people seeking my services and/or products. I am successful in my field.

Today I get UP, think UP, cheer UP, bounce back UP, measure UP, keep UP, save UP, reach UP, polish UP, open UP, step UP... but I never give up!

DIAMOND QUOTATIONS

"If your outlook on life is negative... your challenges will grind you down. If your outlook on life is positive... your challenges will polish you up."

"The world expects results. Don't tell others about your labor pains in life. Just show them the baby."

"Self-pity is no excuse for inaction in your life. Cancel your pity party. Most people don't care, and the rest are glad it's you and not them."

"Plan TODAY for God's call TOMORROW."

"What you do today had better be important to you because you're giving up a day of your life to do it."

"In everything you do, BE ABOVE AVERAGE. Do and give more than is expected. There is no traffic jam on the extra mile."

"One of the biggest mistakes you can make is to believe you are working for someone else."

"You will develop wisdom teeth when you bite off more than you can chew. Keep promises and commitments."

"Lighthouses don't have to ring bells to call attention to their light. They just shine."

"The only people to get even with... are those who help you."

"Any goal not written down... is just a wish."

"When you stumble... don't crumble. Character is not made in a crisis... it is revealed."

"Don't push your child, lead your child."

"Children watch our examples more than they listen to us."

"The greatest gift you can give others is the example of your own life working. Your success is a gift to others."

"Look in the mirror to meet the only person who really can stop you permanently. Others can only stop you temporarily."

"In life you are either climbing or sliding. If you want to climb mountains, you can't complain about the pebbles in your shoes along the way."

"Fear + action = courage. Courage is the ability to let go of the familiar."

"Our anxiety in a relationship comes from unrealistic or uncommunicated expectations. Don't take someone to the **altar** to **alter** them. If you require a person to change, you require that person to lie to you."

"A marriage has a greater chance of success if 3 books are shared; **cookbook, checkbook and the Good Book.**"

"We train others how to treat us based on our own self-worth and self-esteem."

"Some people build walls instead of bridges."

"When love is real, it heals. Love is a pain killer."

"When your true feelings are suppressed, love cannot be expressed."

"If you don't heal your emotional wounds, you will hurt and harm yourself or others."

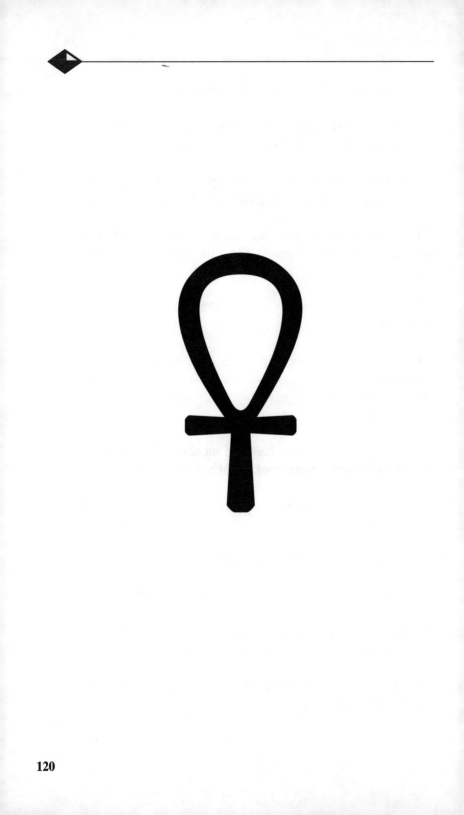

"Your body will present its bill, if you don't take care of its ills."

"Reality is subject to change without notice. Be proactive in your life vs. reactive. Prepare and plan... yet learn when its time to just go with the flow without drowning in the process."

"When a piece of coal undergoes pressure, a beautiful diamond is the result. What happens when you are under pressure? Adversity can make you stronger. You can become **bitter or better**."

"You decide, and God will provide."

"If you work and **apply** yourself, God will **supply** your needs."

"A relationship is in danger when one is so busy working to earn their salt that they forget their sugar."

"Practice an attitude of gratitude."

"If you feel far from God, guess who moved?"

"Are you searching for rocks or diamonds? Be specific with your goals."

"Realize that faith is a verb... not a noun. Faith is to be lived not just talked about. One of my greatest revelations is "Talk is cheap... you have to leap."

"We all live in a tent. Do you live in con**tent** or discon**tent**? Learn how to develop inner peace."

"The universal law fulfills our desires and dreams, OR it fulfills our worries and fears. Be careful of what you think about all day. Be careful what you ask for. God is eavesdropping on your **internal** conversations."

"Be patient and positive. Don't think that God has lost your file. Are you going to <u>lose</u> your faith or <u>use</u> your faith?"

"Parenthood is the art of bringing UP children without putting them DOWN."

"The best thing to spend on your child is your time."

"The factory that produces the most important product in the community is the home."

Possessions do not bring happiness, but happiness does bring possessions.

Obstacles are what you see when you take your eyes off your goal.

My interest is in the future because I'm going to spend the rest of my life there.

Death whispers in my ear, "Live, for I am coming." For those who have lived, they fear not death. So I want to live until I die.

Love looks forward.
Hate looks back.
Anxiety has eyes all over the head.

It's not just what you think, it's how you think.

When I worry, I practice atheism.

What you are seeking,
is also seeking you.

Love is a friendship that is on fire.

In life, you can only go as far as your knowledge and faith will take you.

MY FAVORITE QUOTES FROM THE PAST AND PRESENT

"Big Mama (Grandmother) always said to me, 'Once a task you've first begun, never finish until it's done. Be the labor great or small, do it well or not all all.'"

Tavis Smiley

"Let nothing come between you and the Light."

Thoreau

"Who is more foolish? A child afraid of the dark or man afraid of the Light?"

Unknown

"A person of related mind comes to us softly and gently and easily, so nearly intimately as if it were the blood in our veins. We are utterly relieved and refreshed; it is a sort of joyful solitude."

Emerson

"Don't let your dreams take flight, for everybody knows dreams are stuff from which great deeds and goodness flow.
Don't let your dreams take flight or let one dream grow cold, for when your dreams have died, you've pre-condemned your soul.
Don't let your dreams take flight.
Losing one dream is sin; and if your dreams have fled, go get them back again."

Perry Tanksley

"Modern man is so much a part of a crowd, that he is dying of personal loneliness."

Albert Einstein

"Only by much searching and mining are gold and diamonds obtained and man can find every truth connected with his being... if he will dig deep into the mine of his soul; and know that he is the maker of his character, the molder of his life and the builder of his destiny."

James Allen

"Joy is finding your direction, not just your destination."

Unknown

"If you believe in your Divine Destiny, nothing else matters. Your conquering, positive desire will overcome all obstacles. Your life will be molded according to your belief and vision. Not a hair on your head will be harmed until your life mission has been filled."

A. K. Mozumdar

"Trust your instinct to the end, though you can render no reason. It is in vain to hurry it. By trusting it to the end, it shall ripen into truth, and you shall know why you believe."

Emerson

"Two birds disputed about a kernel, when a third swooped down and carried it off."

African Proverb (Zaire)

"The peaceful... are the strong."

Oliver Wendell Holmes

"Age is a matter of mind
if you don't mind
it doesn't matter."

Unknown

"Instead of finding faults with others, we should try to cultivate understanding of them. Of course, we can hardly expect that we will get along with everyone, all the time unconditionally. Our world environment is like a polishing machine, into which are thrown may different kinds of rocks, opals, topazes and other precious stones. The machine is filled with water and polishing agents; it turns and churns and rubs. Finally, after so many days, out come beautiful polished jewels.

In this world we are thrown together with all our shortcomings, bad habits, poor attitudes, and we rub against each other to smooth off the rough edges in our character, so that someday we may all be *polished individuals*."

Brother Premamoy

"To effect the quality of a day is the highest of arts."

Thoreau

"There is pain in staying the same and there is pain in change. Pick the one that moves you forward."
                                        Earnie Larsen

"Not everything that is faced can be changed. But nothing can be changed until it is faced."
                                        James Baldwin

"The unreflected life is not worth living."
                                        Socrates

"Life is a great big canvas and you should throw all the paint on it you can."
                                        Danny Kaye

"Love consists in this, that two solitudes protect, touch and greet each other."
                                        Rainer Maria Rike

"Love before, love behind, love above, love below, love all around, love will lay hatred down."
                                        Navajo prayer

"We must always change, renew and rejuvenate ourselves, otherwise we harden."
                                        Goethe

"Faith is going to the edge with all we have and know
and taking one MORE step."

Unknown

" 'Come to the edge,' he said.
They said, 'We are afraid.'
'Come to the edge,' he said.
They came.
He pushed them
and they flew."

Guillaume Apollinaire

"From the moment we set foot on the spiritual path, nothing
happens by coincidence."

Paramahansa Yogananda

"God attracts you with a certain sweetness, much like falling
in love."

GEO Magazine

"The spiritual journey is to go deeper into yourself, making
more room for God to enter."

GEO Magazine

"It is all with God. He is gracious and merciful. His way is in Love, through which we all are. Wherever and whoever you are, always strive to follow and walk in the right Path and ask for aid and assistance... herein lies the ultimate and eternal happiness which is ours through His grace."

"Ohnedaruth" John Coltrane

"Teachers can open the door, but you must enter by yourself."

Chinese Proverb

"Ring the bells that still can ring.
Forget your **perfect** offering.
There is a crack in everything.
That's how the light gets in."

Leonard Cohen

"When the student is ready, the Master appears."

Buddhist Proverb

"Losers visualize the penalties of failure.
Winners visualize the rewards of success."

Dr. Rob Gilbert

"Follow your bliss."

Joseph Campbell

"To conquer fear is the beginning of wisdom."
Bertrand Russell

"One who fears failure limits his activities. Failure is only the opportunity to **begin again more intelligently**."
Henry Ford

"Many of life's failures are people who did not realize how close they were to success when they gave up."
Thomas Edison

"We should read for power. The book should be a ball of light in one's hand."
Ezra Pound

"Nothing in the world can take the place of persistence.
Talent will not;
nothing is more common than unsuccessful men with talent.
Genius will not;
un-rewarded genius is almost a proverb.
Education alone will not;
the world is full of educated derelicts.
Persistence and determination alone are omnipotent."
Calvin Coolidge

"You may have to fight a battle more than once to win it."
Margaret Thatcher

"God gives every bird its food, but He does not throw it into the nest."

J. G. Holland

"Rain does not fall on one roof alone."

African Proverb (Cameroon)

"Two birds disputed about a kernel, when a third swooped down and carried it off."

African Proverb (Zaire)

"Advise and counsel him; if he does not listen, let adversity teach him."

African Proverb (Ethiopia)

"The opportunity that God sends does not wake up him who is asleep."

African Proverb (Senegal)

"If a centipede loses a leg, it does not prevent him from walking."

African Proverb (Senegal)

Inspirational speaker and author, Jewel Diamond Taylor, is the founder of the personal development organization, THE ENLIGHTENED CIRCLE, founded in 1985 in the Los Angeles, California area. The mission and vision of this life enrichment service are to practice, seek, know and share positive knowledge and information.

THE ENLIGHTENED CIRCLE offers the experiences of networking, classes, workshops, rites of passage, retreats and conferences.
To learn more about upcoming events, membership, "Positive Talk" news-letter subscription, meetings in your area or to inquire about speaker avail-ability for your organization, corporation, conference, campus, church, bookclub or retreat....call/write:

> Jewel Diamond Taylor
> 4195 Chino Hills Pkwy. #180
> Chino Hills, CA   91709
> (323) 964-1736
> (323) 954-4070 (positive thought for the day)
> e.mail: jeweldiam@aol.com
> www.jeweldiamondtaylor.com

Other Products from Quiet Time Publishing

 Success Gems *Your Personal Motivational Success Guide* by Jewel Diamond Taylor ISBN: 1884743 013 ($12.00)

 Sisterfriends *Empowerment for Women and a Celebration of Sisterhood* by Jewel Diamond Taylor ISBN: 1884743 064 ($12.99)

God Made Me Beauty-full *Building Self-Esteem in African American Women* by Terri McFaddin ISBN: 1884743-056 ($12.00)

 Coming September 1999:
Jewel Diamond Taylor's *Success Journal*
The All new *Success Pak* (Prosperity Action Kit)
Call or write Quiet Time Publishing for more details

Available at your local bookstore or to ship, please include $3.00 for the first item and $1.00 for each additional item.
Send check or money order payable to:
Quiet Time Publishing
1633 Bond Avenue,
East St. Louis, Illinois 62207
(618) 875-6808
Illinois & California residents, please add 8.25% sales tax.